How to Research Congress

How to Research Congress

Fenton S. Martin
Robert U. Goehlert
Indiana University

Congressional Quarterly Inc.
Washington, D.C.

Copyright © 1996 Congressional Quarterly Inc., 1414 22nd Street, N.W., Washington, D.C. 20037

Printed in the United States of America

Library of Congress Cataloging-in-Publication Data

Martin, Fenton S.
   How to research Congress / Fenton S. Martin, Robert U. Goehlert.
     p.   cm.
   Includes bibliographical references and indexes.
   ISBN 0-87187-870-4 — ISBN 0-87187-869-0 (pbk.)
   1. United States.   Congress—Information services.   2. Legislative bodies—Research—United States.   I. Goehlert, Robert.   II. Title.
JK1108.M349   1996
328.73'0072—dc20   96-3867
                                                 CIP

Contents

Preface

How to Research Congress provides an introduction to basic research resources on Congress. Our objective is to acquaint the researcher with the various types of resources available for studying Congress. Some are specific guides to finding or interpreting statutes; others are general guides to congressional and legal resources. We also include information on materials that provide background data on Congress and current events. We have been selective in the resources included, and the annotations have been kept as simple as possible.

The first part of this book covers secondary sources and the finding tools used to locate them. These sources, including almanacs, atlases, dictionaries, encyclopedias, handbooks, and biographies are important in providing background and historical information. In addition, news publications, including newspapers, newsmagazines, news services, and journals, provide current information on Congress. Pertinent indexes, abstracting services, online databases, and CD-ROM products are also described. These publications and services are key not only in pinpointing specific information, but also in simplifying the research process.

The second part of this book covers primary sources and the finding tools used to locate them. First, we describe various guides for researching Congress. These guides offer overviews of the type and variety of congressional publications available to the researcher. This is followed by a discussion of references that are useful in finding information about Congress. We also note available sources useful in locating case law and administrative law, both of which are integral to legal research.

The third part contains a selected bibliography of major books about Congress. They offer information on its history, development, powers, and relations with the other branches of the federal government. We have also provided a glossary of congressional terms, an author index, and a title index.

We wish to thank the Political Science Department at Indiana University for its support of our research. Thanks to Steve Flinn (Systems Manager) for his technical assistance. Special thanks go to Richard L. Pacelle, Jr., for the many helpful suggestions he made about the research guide and for the time he spent answering questions about Congress. We appreciate the excellent job Tracy Villano, our copy editor, did making corrections, rewording paragraphs, and seeing that citations were complete.

How to Research Congress

Introduction

There is no single best approach to the study of Congress. Each approach relies upon a distinct body of literature that can be used to develop a topic and formulate a research strategy. Most important, the approach taken can shape the focus of the research. For example, a legal analysis might emphasize the statutory history, whereas an institutional approach might focus on organizational behavior. In each case the kind of literature drawn upon, both primary and secondary sources, will vary. And because not every library will have all the sources cited in this book, you must consider what resources are available before setting out to conduct research on any topic related to Congress.

Types of Legal Resources

Legal resources can be divided into three categories: primary sources, secondary sources, and finding tools. They include books, articles, databases, newspapers, indexes, reference tools, and CD-ROMs. Some sources contain more than one type of information. They may include both primary and secondary sources and be finding tools at the same time.

Primary legal sources are publications by government bodies. These include legislative documents, judicial opinions and reports, administrative regulations, rules, and decisions. Primary legal sources range in time from the first laws to the most recent statutes. Since primary legal sources are enforced until they are overruled or repealed, it is important that even the earliest primary legal sources remain accessible.

Secondary legal sources are materials about the law that are used to explain, interpret, and update primary sources. They can be interpretive, analytical, or critical in nature. These include legislative histories, commentaries and surveys, administrative reports, briefs and opinions, dictionaries, encyclopedias, and periodicals. Secondary legal sources can sometimes be used as finding tools to l   her sources.

Finding tools are intended to help locate or update primary and secondary sources. They include indexes to congressional publications and research guides. Because most primary legal sources are issued chronologically, the researcher needs some means of subject access into this large body of literature. Without a subject approach to legal sources, it is difficult to find existing statutes. Most finding tools provide subject access. This includes encyclopedias; research guides; bibliographies; indexes to statutes, cases, and decisions; periodical indexes; and online database services such as LEXIS/NEXIS, WESTLAW, CQ'S WASHINGTON ALERT, and LEGI-SLATE.

Designing a Research Strategy

The research strategy you develop can determine the kinds of materials you seek. In this section, we present an outline on how to develop a topic and design a research strategy on Congress.

Developing a topic that is sufficiently narrow, manageable, and original is not an easy task. Most often topics grow from some unanswered question that may warrant further analysis and explanation. If you have an idea about something to investigate, you are well on your way. If you do not come across some statement you question or think needs elaboration, then you must create a topic. One method is to browse through current newspapers, books, bibliographies, or a periodical index to see what is being written about Congress. Preliminary research and reading can help you develop a topic. You should look for an interesting bill or law that you would like to analyze, evaluate, or comment on. Then do some initial research to see what books and articles have been written about that particular topic.

During your preliminary research, develop questions regarding the particular bill or law. This may involve combining one law with another or combining a statute with a concept. As you develop a topic, keep in mind that eventually you will need to define a proposition or hypothesis to prove or disprove. You should also think about describing the topic, such as when it took place, who was involved, why it was considered a problem, who was affected, and so on. The more you think about a topic and outline the details, the easier it will be later to search thoroughly and systematically for material.

Remember that secondary sources, such as encyclopedias, dictionaries, or journal articles, can be useful in starting your research as well as in directing you to important primary sources. Write down any bills, statutes, important committees and subcommittees, and members of Congress cited in the secondary sources.

Once you have a topic but before you begin to search for additional materials, you should think through a basic research design. This will help you organize your research strategy and clarify the topic. If the topic is too broad, it will become apparent. If a proposition cannot be argued effectively, you will have to select another hypothesis. A research design should include a statement of the topic, a review of the literature, a definition of the hypothesis to be tested, a description of the operational design, and the methods of analysis and interpretation.

Before conducting a research strategy, develop a checklist of the kinds of materials you are looking for and the specific finding tools necessary to gain access to those materials. This includes identifying what significant facts and issues need to be researched. Creating a logical outline of issues and subissues can be extremely useful in defining a research strategy. As your outline changes, so will your research strategy. It is also important to think of which disciplines, such as law, history, or political science, you might explore for materials, as well as the period you will cover (one year, a decade). Outlining such a research strategy ahead of time will make your library search more efficient and productive.

1. Search the library's subject catalog.

2. Search periodical indexes and abstracting services, either in print, on CD-ROMs, or online format.

3. Search online information services, such as LEXIS/NEXIS, CQ'S WASHINGTON ALERT, LEGI-SLATE, and WESTLAW.

4. Search on the Internet for any pertinent background information and government documents.

5. Search encyclopedias and dictionaries for background information and citations to primary sources.

6. Search newspaper indexes for information on the topic.

7. Search for bibliographies on the specific topic.

8. Search research guides to identify any special compilations, bibliographies, and other finding tools particularly germane to the topic.

9. Check bibliographies and footnotes in books, articles, dissertations, and other materials you will use to begin your research. These can lead to important secondary sources.

10. Make a list of primary sources, including bills, committee hearings and reports, debates, and statutes, identified through secondary sources. Also write down the dates when actions occurred and who was involved.

11. Search the appropriate finding tools for identifying congressional and other government documents.

12. Gather and analyze the documents.

When designing a research strategy, it is important to make a checklist of all of the possible terms, concepts, and names that you will check for as subject headings. Such a list may include as many as a dozen or more possible subject headings. Since subject headings vary in subject catalogs, encyclopedias, and other finding tools, think of synonyms to use from one finding tool to another. As you conduct a research strategy, you will find which subject headings are most useful. But it is better to search under a variety of subject headings rather than just one or two. A common mistake is to look only under one or two subject headings, find only a few citations, and assume that little has been written about a topic. While that may be the case, many times the materials are indexed under other subject headings. If you are using tools that allow you to perform key word searching, keep track of what terms you use for searching. If you are using tools that have subject and key word searching, try both approaches.

It is important to keep track of which finding tools you have checked and the subject headings and key words you have used. Keeping a record of your research makes it easier to revise your strategy and remember which finding tools are available, especially if you need to refer back to a source to get additional citations or information. The most important thing to do when conducting a search is to take notes and make a record of where you find a particular citation. Keeping a record of the finding tools searched (such as which volumes or years or which subject headings) will save you time and facilitate the writing of your research.

Secondary Sources and Finding Tools

This section identifies a selected list of reference books and services that are useful in conducting research on Congress. The research sources are grouped by category, and short descriptions are provided for many of the sources.

Almanacs

Most almanacs can be used as ready reference sources. While every almanac uses a different format, they all contain similar information.

Congressional Quarterly Almanac. Washington, DC: Congressional Quarterly, 1945— .
This annual work summarizes the previous year's congressional actions. Included are accounts of major legislation enacted, a summary of presidential programs and initiatives, analyses of Supreme Court decisions, the results of any federal elections held during the year, an examination of lobbying activities, and other special reports.

Congressional Yearbook. Washington, DC: Congressional Quarterly, 1994— .
This annual work summarizes each session of Congress. Topics covered include the year's important issues, legislative accomplishments, and political and election events. This reference provides a good starting point for research on a particular event, issue, policy, or piece of legislation.

Congress and the Nation. 8 vols. Washington, DC: Congressional Quarterly, 1945–1993.

This reference set, with an additional volume added every four years, is a well-organized work that affords quick access to descriptions of major legislation and issues in the Congress, White House, and Supreme Court. The set provides an excellent chronological history of major legislative programs and political developments during each Congress and executive administration and offers biographical data as well as information on major votes, key judicial decisions, and election issues.

Dole, Robert J. *Historical Almanac of the United States Senate.* Washington, DC: U.S. Government Printing Office, 1989.

This volume contains three hundred "Bicentennial Minutes" presented by Bob Dole (R-Kan) on the floor of the Senate. Included are anecdotes about individuals, events, and the origin of Senate practices and procedures. The "minutes" are arranged in chronological order.

Atlases

These three atlases graphically document the history of apportionment and redistricting and illustrate changes in social trends in congressional districts. The atlases provide a unique perspective from which to analyze congressional voting and the growth of party politics.

Martis, Kenneth C. *Historical Atlas of Political Parties in the United States Congress,* 1789–1989. New York: Macmillan, 1989.

Martis, Kenneth C. *The Historical Atlas of the United States Congressional Districts,* 1789–1983. New York: Free Press, 1983.

Martis, Kenneth C., and Gregory A. Elmes. *The Historical Atlas of State Power in Congress,* 1790–1990. Washington, DC: Congressional Quarterly, 1993.

Biographical Directories

These tools direct a researcher to information about members of Congress and their staff, committee staff, and other key government officials. In addition to the printed guides listed below, biographical information about members of Congress can be found on both the Internet and the on-line databases (discussed later).

Barone, Michael, and Grant Ujifusa. *The Almanac of American Politics.* Washington, DC: National Journal, 1972— .
This biennial guide is arranged alphabetically by state. An intro-ductory description of the state's political background precedes sketches of the state's delegates that offer information on members' backgrounds and ideologies, the committees they serve on, their records on key votes, their electoral histories, and ratings of mem-bers by interest groups. Also included are political profiles of each congressional district that offer census data, federal outlay figures, tax burdens, and demographics. *The Almanac of American Politics* is available online through LEGI-SLATE and LEXIS/NEXIS.

Biographical Directory of the United States Congress, 1774–1989: Bicentennial Edition. Washington, DC: U.S. Government Printing Office, 1989.
This directory provides short biographies, arranged alphabeti-cally, of senators and representatives who served in Congress from 1774 to 1989. Also included are a chronological list of execu-tive officers of administrations from 1789 to 1989, a list of dele-gates to the Continental Congress, and a list of congresses by date and session.

Congressional Staff Directory. Mount Vernon, VA: Staff Directories, Ltd., 1959— .
This directory lists the staffs of each member of Congress and of the committees and subcommittees of both houses, and gives short biographical sketches of key staff personnel. The committee and subcommittee assignments of members' staff are listed, as are the names of key federal officials and their liaison staffs. An index of personal names offers quick access to specific indi-viduals. The *Congressional Staff Directory* is published every May and October and is available from the publisher on disk as Congressional Staff Directory on Disk. Staff Directories Limited publishes the *Congressional Staff Directory* on CD-ROM, which includes in addition the *Federal Staff Directory* and the *Judicial Staff Directory.* The company also publishes a Member Data Disk that offers over 150 fields of ASCII data, including education, military service, work experience, district office data, and com-mittees and subcommittees, among others. The *Congressional Staff Directory* is available online through LEXIS/NEXIS and LEGI-SLATE.

Politics in America: Members of Congress in Washington and at Home. Washington, DC: Congressional Quarterly, 1980— .
This biennial directory provides an overview of members of Congress. Included are each member's birth date, education, military career, family information, religion, political career, and address. Members' legislative influence, personal styles, election data and campaign finances, voting records, and interest group ratings are given as well. The directory provides profiles and maps of each congressional district and lists the membership of Senate and House committees and subcommittees. *Politics in America 1996* provides a CD-ROM version of the book that adds information from *Congressional Districts in the 1990s. Politics in America* is available online through CQ'S WASHINGTON ALERT.

U.S. Congress. *Official Congressional Directory.* Washington, DC: U.S. Government Printing Office. 1809— .
This biennial directory contains biographical and statistical information about current members of Congress. Included is information about party membership, birth dates and places, education, military career, religion, memberships, occupations, political careers, and family. The directory also provides information about members' state delegations, terms of service, and committee memberships and offers a tally of votes cast for each member in congressional elections. A discussion of congressional sessions, maps of congressional districts, and an index by name of individual are included as well.

The following works provide similar information:

The Almanac of the Unelected: Staff of the U.S. Congress. . . . Washington, DC: Almanac of the Unelected, Inc., 1988— .

Congressional Yellow Book: Who's Who in Congress, Including Committees and Key Staff. New York: Leadership Directories, 1977— .

Who's Who in Congress. Washington, DC: Congressional Quarterly, 1991— .

Dictionaries

Dictionaries on Congress can be useful in finding ready answers to basic reference questions. Dates, terms, concepts, definitions, procedures, rules, and information about individuals are easily accessed with dictionaries.

Dickson, Paul, and Paul Clancy. *The Congress Dictionary: The Ways and Meanings of Capitol Hill.* New York: Wiley, 1993.

Elliot, Jeffrey M., and Sheikh R. Ali. *The Presidential Congressional Political Dictionary.* Santa Barbara, CA: ABC-Clio, 1984.

Kravitz, Walter. *Congressional Quarterly's American Congressional Dictionary.* Washington, DC: Congressional Quarterly, 1993.

Handbooks

Handbooks usually offer a collection of essays, written by experts in the field that provide overviews of various aspects of the subject under study.

Lowenberg, Gerhard, Samuel C. Patterson, and Malcolm E. Jewel, comps. *Handbook of Legislative Research.* Cambridge, MA: Harvard University Press, 1985.
This excellent volume summarizes the state of research on the U.S. Congress and other legislative bodies. It offers discussions on the organization, development, and procedural workings of legislative bodies as well as on elections, campaigning, the media, and relations with other branches of government. This handbook is especially useful in identifying key writings on various aspects of Congress.

Encyclopedias

Encyclopedias aid the researcher in locating basic information, such as dates, names, and significant events. The following excellent encyclopedias on Congress can be used to find facts and explanations of procedures and processes.

Bacon, Donald C., Roger H. Davidson, and Morton Keller, eds. *Encyclopedia of the United States Congress.* New York: Simon and Schuster, 1994.
This four-volume set contains more than one thousand original essays on the Congress. The encyclopedia is fully cross-referenced with bibliographies following each article and a comprehensive

index of terms, concepts, and names. This is the definitive encyclopedia on the history, structure, politics, and culture of the
Congress.

Congress A to Z: Congressional Quarterly's Ready Reference Encyclopedia. 2d
ed. Washington, DC: Congressional Quarterly, 1993.
This volume contains approximately thirty core essays that
provide an overview of Congress, including its structures and
powers, leadership, voting, finance, and budgeting process. The
core essays are supplemented by almost 250 entries not covered
in the broader essays. These include definitions of terms, profiles
of individual committees, and biographies of selected members,
both past and present. The entries are arranged alphabetically
and cross-referenced. The encyclopedia includes extensive indexes and appendices.

Silbey, Joel, ed. *Encyclopedia of the American Legislative System: Studies of the
Principle Structures, Processes, and Policies of Congress and State Legislatures Since the Colonial Era.* New York: Scribner's, 1994.
This three-volume set includes ninety-one essays organized into
six sections. The work is fully cross-referenced and each essay
includes a bibliography. In most cases, Congress is dealt with
as a single entry, though occasionally an essay will analyze the
various legislative levels together. The work covers the history,
membership, process, powers, behavior, and major policy issues
of Congress.

Bibliographies

The bibliographies in this section cover a variety of resources, including books, journal literature, dissertations, and selected government
documents.

Goehlert, Robert U., and Fenton S. Martin. *The United States Congress: An
Annotated Bibliography, 1980–1993.* Washington, DC: Congressional
Quarterly, 1994.
This annotated bibliography includes 3,200 citations to books,
journal articles, research reports, dissertations, and selected documents. The citations are classified according to fourteen major topics: history and development of Congress, congressional process,
reform of Congress, powers of Congress, congressional investigations, foreign affairs, committees, legislative analysis, legislative

case studies, leadership in Congress, pressures on Congress, Congress and the electorate, members of Congress, and the support of Congress. This work is a companion volume to the next entry. By using both bibliographies, a researcher can identify all the books, articles, and dissertations written about Congress through 1993.

Goehlert, Robert U., and John R. Sayre. *The United States Congress: A Bibliography.* New York: Free Press, 1982.
This bibliography on Congress includes 5,620 citations to books, journal articles, research reports, dissertations, and selected documents. The citations are classified according to fourteen major topics: history and development of Congress, congressional process, reform of Congress, powers of Congress, congressional investigations, foreign affairs, committees, legislative analysis, legislative case studies, leadership in Congress, pressures on Congress, Congress and the electorate, members of Congress, and the support of Congress. This work is a companion volume to the preceding entry. By using both bibliographies, a researcher can identify all the books, articles, and dissertations written about Congress through 1993.

Goehlert, Robert U., Fenton S. Martin, and John R. Sayre. *Members of Congress: A Bibliography.* Washington, DC: Congressional Quarterly, 1996.
This bibliography offers an extensive listing of scholarly biographical references to individuals who served in the U.S. Congress since 1774. While not all members are represented, for those who are citations to books, articles, dissertations, and essays within edited volumes about their public and private lives are featured.

Kennon, Donald R., ed. *The Speakers of the U.S. House of Representatives: A Bibliography, 1789–1984.* Baltimore: Johns Hopkins University Press, 1986.
This specialized bibliography is arranged in chronological order by Speaker. For each Speaker there is a brief biographical profile followed by a listing of manuscript collections. A bibliography of books, dissertations, and articles about and by each Speaker is also provided. The work includes a subject and author index.

Indexes

Indexes and abstracting services are crucial for finding journal articles on Congress. Many indexes are now available on CD-ROM, which can save time and effort. The following printed indexes are the most useful for finding journal articles pertaining to Congress.

ABC POL SCI: A Bibliography of Contents: Political Science and Government. Santa Barbara, CA: ABC-Clio, 1969— .
The tables of contents of journals, both U.S. and foreign, appear six times a year in this index. Because it is published in advance of the journals' publications dates, the index is especially useful for finding very recent articles on the Congress. It is available on CD-ROM and as an online database.

America: History and Life. Santa Barbara, CA: ABC-Clio, 1964— .
Articles, book and film reviews, and dissertations are covered in this serial bibliography. A streamlined format adopted in 1989 offers quarterly indexes containing abstracts and citations. There is also a cumulative annual index. This abstracting service provides excellent coverage of materials in history, political science, and the social sciences in general. You should always include this index when doing historical research on Congress. It is available on CD-ROM and as an online database.

Current Law Index. Menlo Park, CA: Information Access Corp., 1980— .
This monthly paper index covers legal periodicals and newspapers. Its microfilm counterpart, *Legal Resources Index*, cumulates the information found in the paper copy. *Legal Resources Index* is available on CD-ROM, where it is called LegalTrac. This index should be consulted for any literature search on the Congress.

Humanities Index. New York: H. W. Wilson, 1974— .
This is a quarterly index to English-language journals in the humanities. The articles are indexed by author and subject. This index covers the major history journals and is best used in searches for citations related to the history of the Congress. It is available on CD-ROM and as an online database.

Index to Legal Periodicals. New York: H. W. Wilson, 1908— .
This monthly work indexes articles appearing in legal periodicals of the United States, Canada, Great Britain, Northern Ireland, Australia, and New Zealand. Indexes are provided for authors, subjects, book reviews, and cases. This index should be used in almost every literature search on the Congress. Since it is one of the oldest legal indexes, it can be used for historical research as well. *Index to Legal Periodicals* is available on CD-ROM and as an online database.

International Political Science Abstracts. Paris: International Political Science
  Association. 1951— .
  This bimonthly work abstracts articles published in English-
  language and foreign-language political science journals. The abstracts of the English-language articles appear in English, and the
  abstracts of the foreign-language articles appear in French. This
  is the best source for finding foreign-language articles about the
  Congress. Even if you are not interested in foreign-language material, you should check to see if this service has citations on the
  Congress that have not appeared in other indexes. *International
  Political Science Abstracts* is available on CD-ROM.

Public Affairs Information Service Bulletin (PAIS). New York: PAIS, 1915— .
  This weekly subject guide to American politics indexes government publications, books, and periodical literature. It indexes the
  *National Journal, Congressional Quarterly Weekly Report, Congres-
  sional Digest,* and, selectively, the *Weekly Compilation of Presidential
  Documents. PAIS* is cumulated quarterly and annually and is
  available on CD-ROM and as an online database.

Reader's Guide to Periodical Literature. New York: H. W. Wilson, 1905— .
  Articles in popular periodicals published in he United States are
  indexed in this semimonthly guide. The articles are indexed by
  author and subject. Each yearly cumulation of this index includes
  hundreds of citations about the Congress. The *Reader's Guide* is a
  vital reference tool for researching events within the past year. It
  is available as a CD-ROM product and as an online database.

Social Sciences Citation Index (SSCI). Philadelphia: Institute for Science Information, 1973— .
  The *Social Sciences Citation Index* indexes more journals than any
  other index in the social sciences. Works cited include books,
  journal articles, dissertations, reports, and proceedings. There are
  four separate indexes: a source (author) index, a corporate index,
  a key word subject index, and a citation index. Items appearing in
  the citation index have been cited in footnotes or bibliographies
  in the social sciences. The *Social Sciences Citation Index* has several
  unique features that are helpful for studying the Congress. The
  corporate index allows the user to identify publications issued by
  particular organizations, such as the Brookings Institution. The
  source and citation indexes can be used to identify the writings of
  a particular scholar who has written extensively on the Congress,
  as well as to identify other researchers who have cited these

writings. *SSCI* is published three times a year and cumulated annually. It is available on CD-ROM and as an online database.

Social Sciences Index. New York: H. W. Wilson, 1975— .
This quarterly work indexes articles found in the major journals in political science as well as other social sciences. Every literature search on the Congress, regardless of the topic, should include this index. It is available on CD-ROM and as an online database.

Sociological Abstracts. San Diego, CA: Sociological Abstracts, 1952— .
This is the major abstracting service in the field of sociology. In addition to journals, it indexes papers presented at meetings and book reviews. The entries are arranged in thirty-three major categories. The author and subject indexes are cumulated annually. The service is available on CD-ROM and as an online database.

United States Political Science Documents. Pittsburgh: University Center of International Studies, University of Pittsburgh, 1976— .
The major political science journals are indexed and abstracted in this annual two-volume work. The first volume contains indexes by author, subject, geographic area, proper name, and journal title. The second volume abstracts the articles indexed in the first volume. This is an index that should be used in every search strategy. It is available as an online database.

U.S. Government Periodicals Index. Bethesda, MD: Congressional Information Service, 1994— .
This quarterly index covers journals published by the federal government, including the *CRS Review* and the *GAO Journal.* Access is by subject and author. The first issue of the print index was published in 1994 and covered journals published from October through December 1993. Retrospective annual volumes will provide retrospective coverage to 1988. It is available on CD-ROM and as an online database.

Compact Disk Products

Many reference sources are now being published in the compact disk (CD-ROM) format. Printed indexes previously cited that are in compact disk format are listed here in alphabetical order.

ABC POL SCI on Disc
> This database corresponds to the printed *ABC POL SCI.* It indexes all of the major political science journals. Coverage is from 1984 to the present.

America: History and Life on Disc
> This database corresponds to the printed *America: History and Life.* It indexes journal articles, book reviews, and dissertations. Coverage is from 1984 to the present.

Humanities Index
> This database corresponds to the printed *Humanities Index.* English-language periodicals in history, philosophy, and religion are indexed. Coverage is from 1984 to the present.

Index to Legal Periodicals
> This database corresponds to the printed *Index to Legal Periodicals.* It indexes legal periodicals, yearbooks, and law reviews. Coverage is from 1981 to the present.

International Political Science Abstracts
> This database corresponds to the printed *International Political Science Abstracts.* It includes major journals in political science, public and international law, and international relations. Coverage is from 1989 to the present.

LegalTrac
> This database contains citations to the major law periodicals and to some legal newspapers. Coverage is from 1980 to the present.

PAIS International
> This product includes the *Public Affairs Information Service Bulletin,* which covers publications in public policy, economics, political science, and the social sciences. Coverage is from 1982 to the present.

Reader's Guide to Periodical Literature
> This database, which corresponds to the printed version, indexes general interest magazines and some scholarly journals. Coverage is from 1983 to the present.

Social Sciences Citation Index Compact Disc Edition
> This is a CD-ROM version of the printed *Social Sciences Citation*

Index (SSCI). This product indexes more social science journals than any other single index or CD-ROM product. Coverage is from 1981 to the present.

Social Sciences Index
This CD-ROM version of *Social Sciences Index* indexes English-language periodicals in the social sciences. Coverage is from 1983 to the present.

SocioFile
This CD-ROM subset of the printed *Sociological Abstracts* provides abstracts from all of the major journals in sociology. Coverage is from 1974 to the present.

U.S. Government Periodical Index
This database was published in 1994. It corresponds to the printed *U.S. Government Periodical Index*. Retrospective coverage to 1988 will be included on future disks.

Another CD-ROM product that is of special interest to students of Congress is called InfoTrac. Updated quarterly, InfoTrac provides citations to articles from general interest periodicals as well as scholarly periodicals, including many of the journals and newsmagazines discussed here. Many of the journals indexed on InfoTrac are now available with the full text of the articles.

In addition, there are three CD-ROM products that can be used for identifying U.S. government publications from all branches of the government, including those useful for the study of Congress. These are Government Publications Index on InfoTrac, Government Documents Catalog Subscription Service, and GPO on Silver Platter.

Databases

Online databases are extremely useful because they retrieve information quickly. The following online services are especially helpful for scholars of Congress. These services allow the researcher to obtain information on members and their districts, on committee assignments and committee rosters, on members' voting records and their ratings by outside organizations, on campaign contributions and financing, as well as bill tracking and legislative histories, among other things. A new text on online legal research by Christopher G. Wren and Jill Robinson Wren is especially useful for learning how to search two of the online services. The book, published in 1994 by

Adams and Ambrose, is entitled *Using Computers in Legal Research: A Guide to LEXIS and WESTLAW*. As all of these online services are expensive, be sure to check to see if your library provides access to them for a fee or whether users can access at no charge. (Also, if you are interested in any of the indexes mentioned earlier that are available online, check with a nearby library regarding cost and availability.) The four major online databases are listed below.

CQ'S WASHINGTON ALERT. Washington, DC: Congressional Quarterly. This congressional tracking service provides the full text of successive versions of bills and resolutions; summaries of bills and resolutions prepared by the Congressional Research Service; the full text of committee and conference reports; the full text of the *Congressional Record*; committee and floor schedules; committee and subcommittee action, votes, and rosters; and a listing of roll call votes. The *Congressional Quarterly Weekly Report* is available in full text and information from other CQ publications are in the database, including news from CQ's *Congressional Monitor, CQ Fax Report, Politics in America*, and *CQ Researcher*.

LEGI-SLATE. Washington, DC: LEGI-SLATE. This database tracks and updates congressional and regulatory activity. It provides the full text of bills and resolutions and the full text of the *Congressional Record*. Updates of committee schedules, congressional votes, and the full daily text of the *Federal Register* are offered. There is also a news service with articles from the *National Journal* and the *Washington Post*.

LEXIS/NEXIS. Dayton, OH: Reed Elsevier Inc. This system can be used for finding information about Congress, including bill tracking, floor votes, committee membership, district profiles, member profiles, ratings of members, data from the Federal Election Commission, and analyses from news transcripts such as CNN, ABC, and NPR. LEGIS, one of several "libraries" within the system, is especially useful in obtaining information about Congress. The full text of the *National Journal*, the *Congressional Record*, and the *Almanac of American Politics* are in LEXIS/NEXIS. Numerous legal journals can also be accessed.

WESTLAW. St. Paul, MN: West Publishing Co. This database can be used most effectively for finding citations related to the interpretation of public laws. The database includes access to case law, statutes, administrative materials, legal periodicals, and access to other commercial databases. West publishes

Westlaw Database List, which describes the various databases that comprise WESTLAW, and a student guide entitled *Discovering WESTLAW.*

Journals

While scholarly articles about Congress can be found in many journals, there are several that regularly contain articles about some aspect of congressional politics. These include the *American Journal of Political Science, American Political Science Review, American Politics Quarterly, Journal of Politics, Political Research Quarterly,* and *Polity.* An important new compilation of journal literature on Congress has been published by Carlson Publishing, entitled *The Congress of the United States 1789–1989.* The twenty-three volume set is published in a series of ten titles. The set includes 356 articles that the editors felt should be available to every student and scholar. Each of the ten titles includes a detailed index to the events, individuals, concepts, and topics discussed. The indexes make the set a very comprehensive reference work on Congress.

In addition the four journals listed below deserve special mention because of their focus on Congress.

Congress and the Presidency: A Journal of Capitol Studies. Washington, DC: Center for Congressional and Presidential Studies, American University, 1983— .
This journal covers both Congress and the presidency, interaction between the two, and national policymaking in general. Published twice a year, it contains a mix of articles from both political science and history. Besides research articles, it includes research notes, review essays, and book reviews.

Congressional Quarterly Weekly Report. Washington, DC: Congressional Quarterly, 1945— .
This journal recounts important congressional activities of the previous week, including developments on the floor and in committees. Voting records often accompany coverage of major pieces of legislation. Lobbying activities are given considerable attention, with special reports on the relationship between congressional voting and interest groups. Each issue usually contains several articles on special issues or major legislation pending in Congress. Congressional Quarterly indexes the *Weekly Report* both quarterly and annually. The *Weekly Report* is also indexed in *Public Affairs Information Service Bulletin* and *Social Sciences Index.*

The *Weekly Report* is available online through CQ'S WASHING-
TON ALERT and DATATIMES.

Legislative Studies Quarterly. Iowa City: Comparative Legislative Research
Center, University of Iowa, 1976— .
Although this journal is devoted to the publication of research on
legislatures and parliaments in all settings and across all time
periods, many of the articles deal with the U.S. Congress, especially its processes, history, and behavior. Each issue includes a
Legislative Research Reports section that provides abstracts of
articles on legislative bodies from other scholarly journals. This
section also provides abstracts of papers on legislative studies
presented at the annual meetings of various associations, such as
the American Political Science Association.

National Journal: The Weekly on Politics and Government. Washington, DC:
National Journal, 1969— .
The *National Journal* covers all areas of the federal government. It
provides excellent analyses of the activities of Congress. Each
issue usually contains two or more feature articles on some aspect
of congressional politics. At the end of each issue there is a detailed
index for that issue, as well as an index covering recent weeks.
The *National Journal* is self-indexed by subject semi-annually. It is
also indexed in *Public Affairs Information Service Bulletin. National Journal* is available online through LEXIS/NEXIS and LEGI-
SLATE.

Newsmagazines

Newsmagazines are an excellent source of current information about
Congress. They include news stories, editorials, and feature articles on
Congress. The magazines listed below regularly carry articles on Congress
written from a variety of political viewpoints. The best indexes for finding
articles from newsmagazines are the *Reader's Guide to Periodical Literature*
and InfoTrac. Many of these magazines are available on various online
services such as LEXIS/NEXIS, CQ'S WASHINGTON ALERT, LEGI-
SLATE, and WESTLAW. The online services do change what they carry, so
the best way to determine what magazines they include is to check online.
Although they publish some scholarly articles on Congress, these magazines usually are not thought of as research journals. They are most useful
for keeping up on current events and as a record of public opinion, as evi-
denced in their editorials and opinion articles.

Atlantic Monthly. Boston: Atlantic Monthly Company, 1857— .

CQ Researcher. Washington, DC: Congressional Quarterly, 1991— .

Commentary. New York: American Jewish Committee, 1945— .

Common Cause Magazine. Washington, DC: Common Cause, 1983— .

Congressional Digest. Washington, DC: Congressional Digest, 1922— .

Current. Washington, DC: Heldref Publications, 1960— .

Harper's Magazine. New York: Harper's Magazine Company, 1851— .

Human Events: The National Conservative Weekly. Washington, DC: Human Events, 1944— .

National Review. New York: National Review, 1955— .

New Republic: A Journal of Opinion. Washington, DC: New Republic, 1914— .

Newsweek. New York: Newsweek, 1933— .

Progressive. Madison, WI: Progressive, 1909— .

Society: Social Science and Modern Society. New Brunswick, NJ: Transactions Periodicals Consortium, Rutgers University, 1963— .

Time: The Weekly Newsmagazine. New York: Time-Life, 1923— .

U.S. News and World Report. Washington, DC: U.S. News and World Report, 1933— .

Washington Monthly. Washington, DC: Washington Monthly Company, 1969— .

Newspapers and Indexes

The two best newspapers for following Congress are *The New York Times* and the *Washington Post*. UMI (University Microfilms) has put full text versions of *The New York Times* and the *Washington Post* on CD-ROM starting with 1990. They call these versions NYT on Disc and Washington Post on Disc. The *National Newspaper Index* indexes *The New York Times*, the *Washington Post*, as well as other major newspapers. This microfilm index, available on CD-ROM, is cumulative and updated regularly. Another newspaper that deserves mention is *Roll Call: The Newspaper of Capitol Hill.* Published twice weekly, except for August and two weeks in December, *Roll Call* has become indispensable to observers of Congress not only for its coverage of institutional issues, policy briefings, and reports on candidates and campaigns, but also for its regular guest columns and editorials. *Roll Call* is available in full text on LEXIS/NEXIS beginning in December 1989. Another important news service is *NewsBank*. *NewsBank* indexes selected articles from more than 450 U.S. newspapers, beginning in January 1982. The full text of articles is available on microfiche. The CD-ROM version of this index is called the CD NewsBank and is available as an online database. Another online database is DATATIMES, which indexes both U.S. and international newspapers, news services, and business journals. Especially useful is its indexing of the *Washington Post* and the *Congressional Quarterly Weekly Report*.

Some publishers are now venturing into faxed publications. National Journal's *CongressDaily* is a daily fax publication. It is a concise, five-page report covering the day's news from Congress. It is also available as a print publication and its full text is on LEXIS/NEXIS. Congressional Quarterly also publishes two fax publications, *CQ Fax Report* and *CQ Hill Fax*, both providing current news, legislative action, and statements from members of Congress. You should also remember to check the online services, LEXIS/NEXIS, CQ'S WASHINGTON ALERT, WESTLAW, and LEGI-SLATE to see what newspapers are available there. For example, LEXIS/NEXIS carries *The New York Times* and the *Washington Post* as well as numerous other newspapers.

News Services

Newspaper indexes, whether on CD-ROM or in paper, are sometimes a few weeks behind. Consequently, finding information about a very recent event may not be possible through a search of newspaper indexes. It is important to keep in mind that the online databases, CQ'S WASHINGTON ALERT, LEXIS/NEXIS, LEGI-SLATE, and WESTLAW are especially useful for finding current information, including the previous day's events. These online services include the transcripts of television and radio news broadcasts, as well as many other sources of up-to-date news and analyses.

But if you do not have access to any of the online databases, news services can be most useful since they are only a week or two behind in their publication. *Facts on File: Weekly News Digest and Index* (New York: Facts on File) offers information about very recent events. It is a weekly digest of world events, but the emphasis is on the United States. The entries are grouped under broad topics such as world affairs or national affairs. *Facts on File News* provides a cumulative index and is available on CD-ROM.

A new product published by Research Publications International is Broadcast News on CD-ROM. This product includes transcripts of more than seventy TV and radio news broadcasts found on ABC, CNN, PBS, and NPR, among others. It is updated every month and can be tailored to include only specific stations.

Statistical Sources

In addition to finding data about voting and election returns (which will be discussed later), students and researchers can use statistical sources to locate data about a variety of other congressional activities.

Vital Statistics on Congress. Washington, DC: Congressional Quarterly, 1980– .
This handbook, issued biennially, contains statistical data on Congress as an institution, including membership, elections, campaign financing, committees, staff, workload, operating expenses, budgeting, and voting alignments. The data are historical, with most going back two decades, and some even further.

Another volume, published by Congressional Quarterly, which includes data on Congress as well as the presidency and Supreme Court, is *Vital Statistics on American Politics* (5th ed., 1995).

The fourth volume of Sen. Robert C. Byrd's series, *The Senate, 1789–1989*, is a volume of historical statistics on every facet of the Senate's history, including elections, members, sessions, committees, and leadership. It involves more than one hundred statistical tables with narrative chapter introductions. The fourth volume is entitled *Historical Statistics, 1789–1992* (Washington, DC: U.S. Government Printing Office, 1994).

Primary Sources and Finding Tools

Researching Congress

Researching Congress requires analysis of the legal decisionmaking of all branches of government. The laws, decisions, and rules formulated by the legislative, judicial, and executive branches comprise our pool of legal decisionmaking. In this chapter we focus on three kinds of primary legal sources: statutory law, case law, and administrative law. We also describe the finding tools needed to identify specific laws, cases, and rulings. In addition to reviewing the primary finding tools used to locate congressional documents, we will discuss available sources for finding out about committees' roll call votes, district data, elections, and other aspects of Congress.

Statutory law is the written law enacted by Congress. As a bill passes through Congress, various legislative documents are generated. These documents, which make up a bill's legislative history, are frequently used in legal argument because they show the legislative intent of a statute. Therefore, it is important that you know how to compile a legislative history.

Case law is the law as defined by previously decided cases. You will need to know how to identify and analyze the decisions, oral arguments, and opinions associated with the Supreme Court.

The last source of law is administrative law, which is the rules and orders that interpret statutory law issued by the president, executive departments, administrative agencies, and regulatory commissions. Consequently, you will need to know which finding tools identify, update, and interpret the rules and regulations issued by the executive branch of government.

Doing research on Congress means you must be familiar with all of the branches of government and know how to identify the documents issued by each. After locating the necessary primary and secondary sources you can proceed to analyze the accumulated material.

Guides to Government Publications

The annotated entries listed below are the best guides to government and legal sources, both current and historical. We have listed them in chronological order with the most recently published listed first. Available in most college, university, or public libraries, these guides describe how to find and use government publications and legal finding tools. They are also helpful in that they describe other tools not included here. Because our focus is on current research, we have not cited those guides useful for historical research, especially before World War II. For additional advice on which guides might be helpful, consult a reference or documents librarian.

Lowery, Roger C., and Sue A. Cody. *Political Science: Illustrated Search Strategy and Sources with an Introduction to Legal Research for Undergraduates*. Ann Arbor, MI: Pierian Press, 1993.
This is an excellent guide for students working in the field of political science. The volume includes a good introduction on how to choose a topic and how to find books, articles, and other basic sources. It offers an excellent chapter on locating U.S. government documents and a very detailed chapter on doing legal research. The volume includes numerous illustrations and charts, is well organized, and presents difficult material in an easy to understand format.

Morehead, Joe, and Mary Fetzer. *Introduction to United States Government Information Sources*. 4th ed. Englewood, CO: Libraries Unlimited, 1992.
This work is a valuable guide for anyone interested in researching federal documents. The chapter on legislative branch sources contains a wealth of information. There are separate chapters on the presidency, executive departments, independent agencies, and the judiciary. The book has useful information on how the depository library system works and on the work of the Government Printing Office and Superintendent of Documents. The volume is also useful for learning the technical aspects of documents, such as the SuDocs classification system.

Cohen, Morris L. *Legal Research in a Nutshell.* 5th ed. St. Paul, MN: West Publishing Co., 1992.
This is an excellent, short guide to legal research. It includes chapters on statutes, legislative histories, administrative law, and other aspects of the law. Clear and concise, this book is useful for both the beginner and the skilled researcher.

Jacobstein, J. Myron, and Roy M. Mersky. *Fundamentals of Legal Research.* 5th ed. Westbury, NY: Foundation Press, 1990.
This is a basic text for students learning to do legal research. Those studying Congress will find useful the discussion and explanation of federal legislation and federal legislative histories. A glossary of legal terms and a table of legal abbreviations is also included.

Goehlert, Robert U., and Fenton S. Martin. *Congress and Law Making: Researching the Legislative Process.* 2d ed. Santa Barbara, CA: ABC-Clio Press, 1989.
This volume details how to compile a legislative history using both federal and commercial resources. It offers a thorough discussion of the secondary sources used in researching Congress, including campaigns and elections; identifies relevant dictionaries, encyclopedias, newsmagazines, newsletters, bibliographies, journals, and indexes; and also includes information on finding statistics, archival material, oral histories, television transcripts, and biographical material.

Zwirn, Jerrold. *Congressional Publications and Proceedings: Research on Legislation, Budgets, and Treaties.* 2d ed. Englewood, CO: Libraries Unlimited, 1988.
This volume guides the reader in the role and use of congressional documents in the legislative, budget, and treaty processes. It offers an excellent description and analysis of the internal dynamics of the legislative process and examines the relationship between congressional publications and the legislative process. The work also identifies congressional and nonfederal sources of legislative information resources.

Guides to Congress

Guides are excellent starting points for anyone looking for either the answer to a specific question or an overview of some aspect of the Congress.

Guide to Congress. 4th ed. Washington, DC: Congressional Quarterly, 1991.
   This is the best single volume reference work on Congress.
   Able to answer most general reference questions about Congress,
   the *Guide to Congress* is most valuable to the researcher who is
   seeking a basic, yet thorough understanding of how Congress
   operates. It begins with an account of the origins and history of
   Congress and proceeds with chapters on congressional structure,
   powers and procedures as well as on congressional relations
   with the other branches of government. This edition offers new
   sections on subcommittees, the budget process, redistricting, and
   pay and honoraria.

Woods, Patricia D. *The Dynamics of Congress: A Guide to the People and
   Process in Lawmaking.* Washington, DC: Woods Institute, 1993.
   This work provides an excellent, concise introduction to the legislative process and Capitol Hill. It discusses how a bill becomes
   law, leadership in Congress, the committee system, the congressional hearing process, and congressional staff. This basic guide
   to Congress is clear and easy to understand.

Statutory Law

The effective use of finding tools requires a clear understanding
of how a bill passes through Congress. What follows is a description,
albeit an oversimplified one, of how legislation is passed into law.
A member of one chamber of Congress introduces a bill. The bill is
referred to a committee which then will refer to a subcommittee. The
subcommittee may hold hearings on the bill and amend it. The committee then issues its report. The bill is now ready for floor action, where
it may be debated and amended. If it passes, the bill is sent to the other
chamber, where it goes through the same process. Often, each chamber
is simultaneously working on the same or similar bills. After each
chamber has passed its version of the bill, any differences between the
two versions must be reconciled. This can be achieved by one chamber's agreeing to, or modifying the amendments of the other chamber.
Or the bill may be sent to a conference committee. The conference committee attempts to hammer out a bill acceptable to both bodies. Once
both the House and Senate agree on the specific language, the legislation is sent to the president for approval and signature into law. If the
president vetoes the bill, the Congress may have the option of trying to
override the veto.

FIGURE 1   How a Bill Becomes Law

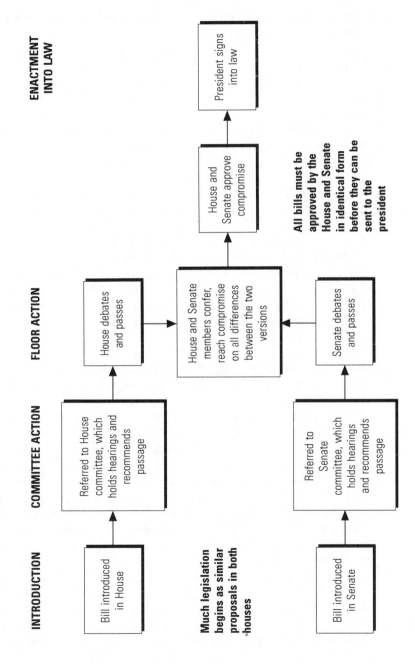

INTRODUCTION   **COMMITTEE ACTION**   **FLOOR ACTION**   **ENACTMENT INTO LAW**

Bill introduced in House

Referred to House committee, which holds hearings and recommends passage

House debates and passes

House and Senate members confer, reach compromise on all differences between the two versions

House and Senate approve compromise

President signs into law

Bill introduced in Senate

Referred to Senate committee, which holds hearings and recommends passage

Senate debates and passes

Much legislation begins as similar proposals in both houses

All bills must be approved by the House and Senate in identical form before they can be sent to the president

Finding Tools

There are numerous finding tools, some published by the federal government and others produced by commercial companies, that are used to trace the course of a bill through Congress and to identify what publications exist. In this section we will describe just a few of the basic sources available. The concise annotations provided do not do justice to these publications, for most are fairly complex. Out intent is not to provide elaborate instructions for their use, but only to acquaint the reader with them and offer some idea of their purpose. Indeed, the best way to gain full knowledge and command of these finding tools is through repeated use. Following this section we include an outline that lists which finding tools to use for tracing legislation

Calendars of the United States House of Representatives and History of Legislation. Washington, DC: U.S. Government Printing Office, 1951— .
   The *Calendars* is published daily when the House is in session. Each Monday there is a subject index to all legislative action to date in both the House and Senate. House and Senate bills passed or pending are arranged numerically in a table. Because this series is cumulative, it is a useful guide to legislative action. There is also information concerning committee schedules and the weekly House floor schedule online on the House Gopher.

CIS/Index: Congressional Information Service/Index toPublications of the United States Congress. Washington, DC: Congressional Information Service, 1970— .
   This is an inclusive monthly index to all congressional publications. It abstracts all forms of publication emanating from the legislative process. Material is indexed by subject, name, committee, bill number, report number, document number, and name of committee chair. Because *CIS/Index* abstracts reports, hearings, and other congressional documents, the researcher can save valuable time by reading the synopses of publications. For most researchers, *CIS/Index* should be the first place to look when tracing legislation. There are quarterly cumulative indexes, and at the end of the year the *CIS/Annual* is issued. Also available are the *CIS Five-Year Cumulative Index 1970–1974, CIS Four-Year Cumulative Index 1975–1978, CIS Four-Year Cumulative Index 1979–1982, CIS Four-Year Cumulative Index 1983–1986, CIS Four-Year Cumulative Index 1987–1990,* and *CIS Four-Year Cumulative Index 1991–1994.* Since 1984 the Congressional Information Ser-

vice has published a *CIS Legislative Histories Annual* that shows exactly what items are included in a law's history, offers full citations, succinctly annotated for the publications in the law's history, and gives a summary of the law's purpose. *CIS/Index* is also available on CD-ROM as Congressional Masterfile II, which indexes all congressional documents indexed in the printed *CIS/Index* since 1970. This includes hearings, committee prints, reports, and documents. Starting in 1995 Congressional Masterfile II will also include *Reports Required by Congress: CIS Guide to Executive Communications* and *Congressional Member Organizations and Caucuses: Publications and Policy Materials.* Congressional Masterfile I provides retrospective indexing to congressional hearings and prints to 1789.

CIS Index to Reports Required by Congress. Washington, DC: Congressional Information Service, 1994— .
Each quarterly issue of this index cumulates material for the year. This index provides detailed information to all numbered executive communications that appear in the *Congressional Record.* This includes various reports from federal departments and agencies that file reports in compliance with statutory requirements. The index provides access by subject, by executive communication and by other document numbers and by the statutory authorities that require the reports to be sent to Congress. CIS also publishes the full text of all the reports on microfiche. Starting in 1995 the *Reports Required by Congress: CIS Guide to Executive Communication* became available on Congressional Masterfile II.

Congress in Print. Washington, DC: Congressional Quarterly, 1977— .
This publication, issued forty-eight times a year, lists all committee hearings, prints, reports, calendars, public laws, and other congressional documents released the previous week. Online access is provided through CQ'S WASHINGTON ALERT.

Congressional Index. Washington, DC: Commerce Clearing House, 1937/38— .
This weekly publication indexes congressional bills and resolutions and lists their current status. The index enables the user to follow the progress of legislation through Congress. It contains a section on voting records in which all roll call votes are reported. Vetoes and subsequent congressional actions are recorded as well.

Congressional Monitor. Washington, DC: Congressional Quarterly, 1965— .
The *Monitor* lists all hearings to be held on the date of issue as well
as those that have been scheduled in the future. Selected press
conferences, speeches, and interest group meetings are listed, and
floor action taken the previous week or scheduled for the current
week is also presented. The *Monitor* offers a two- page summary
of legislative action from the previous day and highlights of
events scheduled to take place the day of issue, and includes committee votes, staff changes, and behind the scenes news. Online
access is provided through CQ'S WASHINGTON ALERT.

Congressional Record: Proceedings and Debates of the Congress. Washington,
DC: U.S. Government Printing Office, 1873— .
This daily record of the proceedings of Congress includes a history
of legislation. It consists of the proceedings of the House, the proceedings of the Senate, extensions, (written submissions and remarks), and the Daily Digest of the activities of Congress. The
proceedings are indexed by subject and name. The *Congressional
Record* is important for finding roll call votes and congressional action on vetoed bills. Prior to the publication of the *Congressional
Record*, the floor proceedings were published in the *Annals of Congress*, the *Register of Debates in Congress*, and the *Congressional Globe*.
The *Congressional Record* is available online through CQ'S WASH-
INGTON ALERT, LEXIS/NEXIS, LEGI-SLATE, and WESTLAW.
The full text of the *Congressional Record* is also on the Internet
through the Library of Congress' MARVEL and THOMAS as well
as GPO ACCESS (see the Internet section for addresses).

Monthly Catalog of United States Government Publications. Washington, DC:
U.S. Government Printing Office, 1895— .
This is an important index for identifying committee hearings
and reports. The *Monthly Catalog* has a subject index as well as an
index arranged by government author. There is also a CD-ROM
version, Government Documents Catalog Subscription Services
(GDCS) which covers the period from 1976 to the present. It can
be searched by author, title, subject, SuDocs Number, and Report
Number. It is much more efficient to use the GDCS than the
printed *Monthly Catalog*.

Public Papers of the Presidents of the United States. Washington, DC: U.S. National Archives and Records Administration, 1958— .
Published annually, the text of these volumes includes oral and
written statements of the presidents. Material is selected from

presidents' communications to Congress, public speeches, press conferences, public letters, messages to heads of state, and executive documents. Bernan Press and Kraus International Publications have published the *Cumulated Indexes to the Public Papers of the Presidents*. At present this ten-volume set includes indexes for the Hoover, Truman, Eisenhower, Kennedy, Johnson, Nixon, Ford, Carter, Reagan, and Bush presidencies. Each volume indexes the complete public papers of the president into one alphabetical listing covering his entire administration. Formerly, it was necessary to use each individual volume of the *Public Papers of the Presidents of the United States*.

United States Code. Washington, DC: U.S. Government Printing Office, 1926— .
The *Code* is a compilation of all federal laws in force. The laws are arranged by subject under fifty "titles." The index volume contains a table of all title and chapter headings and a subject index to all sections. The Superintendent of Documents has issued the U.S. Code on CD-ROM. It includes the current *United States Code* in force on January 2, 1992. This full text CD-ROM provides access to all fifty "titles." You can do very broad subject searches or specific searches for known items. The *United States Code*, starting with the laws of permanent and general effect as of January 1994, is also available on the Internet through GPO ACCESS (see Internet section for addresses).

United States Code Annotated. St. Paul, MN: West Publishing Company, 1927— .
This annual set reprints the *United States Code* and provides extensive annotations, legal notes, analytic comments, and legislative histories. This supplemental material is invaluable for anyone interested in researching the original intent and later interpretation of the statute.

United States Code Congressional and Administrative News. St. Paul, MN: West Publishing Company, 1939— .
This monthly service presents the full text of all public laws and reprints selected House and Senate documents and committee reports. In addition, it provides information on the status of legislation. A particularly useful table provides a legislative history of all bills passed into law. The series is cumulative and it is an excellent tool for legislative tracing.

United States Statutes at Large: Containing the Laws and Concurrent Resolutions Enacted. . . . Washington, DC: U.S. Government Printing Office, 1789—.

The *Statutes at Large* is a record of all laws published in their final form, giving the full text of congressional acts and resolutions passed during a congressional session. Slip laws (the texts of individual acts) are published separately as they are passed and contain legislative histories on their inside back covers.

Weekly Compilation of Presidential Documents. Washington, DC: U.S. Government Printing Office, 1965—.

Published every Monday, this up-to-date source of information covers the activities of the preceding week. It includes the full text of messages, speeches, press conferences, executive orders, and statements made by the president. All bills signed or vetoed are listed and a cumulative index is published with each issue. Weekly press releases and speeches are also on the Internet through the White House home page on the World Wide Web (*http://www.whitehouse.gov/*). For a more detailed discussion of the various types of presidential documents and the finding tools used to identify them, consult Fenton S. Martin and Robert U. Goehlert, *How to Research the Presidency* (Washington, DC: Congressional Quarterly, 1996).

Legislative Histories

Legislation can be traced by obtaining a bill or statute number. Once this is done it is relatively easy to compile a legislative history and identify all of the relevant documents, as most finding tools have bill and statute indexes. If you do not know these numbers, locating them is not difficult. Because most of the finding tools to legislative action are indexed in a variety of ways (for example, by names of individuals, committees, report numbers, and subject), a single piece of information about a bill or law can be used to identify its number. Knowing who introduced a bill or to which committee it was referred can uncover the bill or statute number through use of a name or committee index. If you know no specific information about a bill or law, then it is necessary to use a subject approach. The subject indexing in these guides will generally lead you to the relevant number even if you have only a general knowledge of the substance of a bill or statute.

The outline that follows lists everything that complete legislative history would include.

1. A history of related legislative activities and publications both prior and subsequent to the bill in question.

2. Materials and recommendations made by executive departments concerning the bill.

3. Materials and recommendations made by special interest groups participating in the legislative process.

4. Statements made by sponsors when introducing a bill or statements made by members that were not part of the debate itself.

5. Reports by congressional support agencies.

6. Statements of the president, either messages or comments on signing the bill.

7. Any relevant court cases and decisions that relate to the interpretation of the law.

8. Useful secondary analyses and histories, including journal and newspaper articles. These can be identified by using indexes, CD-ROMs, or online databases, as well as material from:
> *Congressional Quarterly Weekly Report*
> *National Journal*
> *Roll Call: The Newspaper of Capitol Hill*
> *Washington Post*
> *The New York Times*

9. A search on online information services for background information as well as information and documents about the legislation itself. This would include searches on:
> CQ'S WASHINGTON ALERT
> LEGI-SLATE
> LEXIS/NEXIS
> WESTLAW

10. A search on the Internet for background information as well as information about legislation and actual documents themselves. This would include use of:
> THOMAS (*http://thomas.loc.gov*)
> MARVEL (*gopher://marvel.loc.gov*)
> GPO ACCESS (*http://www.access.gpo.gov*)

These sites are especially useful for finding the published versions of bills (starting with the 103d Congress), history of bills (starting with 1994), and the *Congressional Record* (starting with 1994). These sources are also invaluable for finding additional selected pieces of information and documents, including committee schedules and membership, floor schedules, and votes.

11. A chronological account of how a bill has passed, or is currently passing, through Congress that includes dates, committees, actions taken, votes, and an examination of documents relating to its passage. Information can be obtained using the following finding tools:

  a. If a bill is still in Congress, the bill number can be used to determine the present status of the bill through use of:
  Congressional Quarterly Weekly Report
  Congressional Monitor
  Congressional Index—"Bill Status Tables"
  Congressional Record Index—"History of Bills and Resolutions"
  Calendars of the United States House of Representatives and History of Legislation—"History of Bills and Resolutions"

  b. If the bill number or statute number is not known, it can be determined through use of:
  CIS/Index
  Congressional Quarterly Weekly Report
  Congressional Index
  Congressional Record
  Calendars of the United States House of Representatives and History of Legislation

  c. Committee activities and publications, including hearings and prints, can be traced through:
  Congressional Index
  Congressional Quarterly Weekly Report
  Congress in Print
  CIS/Index
  Monthly Catalog of U.S. Government Publications

  d. Sources of committee membership can be found in:
  CIS/Index
  Congressional Staff Directory
  Congressional Index
  Calendars of the United States House of Representatives
  Official Staff Directory
  Politics in America
  Almanac of American Politics

e. Committee reports can be traced through:
   Congressional Index
   Congressional Quarterly Weekly Report
   Congress in Print
   Calendars of the United States House of Representatives and History of Legislation
   CIS/Index
   Monthly Catalog of U.S. Government Publications

f. Floor proceedings and debates can be followed through:
   Congressional Record
   Congressional Quarterly Weekly Report

g. Roll call votes are recorded in:
   Congressional Record
   Congressional Quarterly Weekly Report
   Congressional Roll Call
   Congressional Index
   Also check the online services: CQ'S WASHINGTON ALERT, LEXIS/NEXIS, LEGI-SLATE, WESTLAW.

h. Presidential statements are printed in:
   Weekly Compilation of Presidential Documents
   Public Papers of the President of the United States

i. Slip law approval is indexed in:
   Congressional Record
   Congressional Quarterly Weekly Report
   Weekly Compilation of Presidential Documents
   Congress in Print
   Congressional Index
   Calendars of the United States House of Representatives and History of Legislation
   U.S. Code Congressional and Administrative News

j. Laws are printed in:
   U.S. Code Congressional and Administrative News
   Statutes at Large
   United States Code
   United States Code Annotated

k. Veto messages are indexed in:
   Congressional Record
   Congressional Index
   Congressional Quarterly Weekly Report

CIS/Index
Weekly Compilation of Presidential Documents
Calendars of the United States House of Representatives and History of Legislation

l. Congressional votes on vetoes are recorded in:
Congressional Record
Congressional Index
Congressional Quarterly Weekly Report
Congressional Roll Call

m. If the bill has been passed into law, get the statute number and go to any of the following finding tools to obtain its legislative history:
Slip law—"Legislation History"
Congressional Quarterly Almanac
CIS/Annual—"Legislative Histories"
U.S. Code Congressional and Administrative News—"Table of Legislative History"
Congressional Index—"Bill Status Table"
Calendars of the United States House of Representatives and History of Legislation—"History of Bills and Resolutions"

12. A complete list of documents to be examined would include the following:
   a. The House calendar
   b. The bill as it was introduced in the House
   c. Documents related to the hearings
   d. The bill as it was reported by the House committee
   e. The House committee report
   f. Documents related to the House debate
   g. Legislation as it was passed by the House
   h. The Senate committee report
   i. Documents related to the Senate debate
   j. Senate floor amendments
   k. The Senate-passed version of the legislation
   l. The conference committee print
   m. The conference committee report as it was filed in the Senate
   n. The conference committee report
   o. Presidential messages related to the legislation
   p. The slip law

Because available resources will vary, you should modify this outline to suit your needs, taking into consideration what print and electronic services are accessible to you.

Congressional Information Sources

In addition to the congressional publications that are directly related to the legislative process, there are many other finding tools that can be used to identify primary sources about Congress, including voting, ratings, district data, election returns, and so forth.

Congressional Procedures

The following two guides do an excellent job of explaining the rules, procedures, and terminology used in Congress and provide concise definitions of relevant terms.

CQ's Pocket Guide to the Language of Congress: From Absolute Majority to Zone Whips. Washington, DC: Congressional Quarterly, 1994.

Tiefer, Charles. *Congressional Practice and Procedure: A Reference, Research, and Legislative Guide.* Westport, CT: Greenwood Press, 1989.

The parliamentary procedures used in the House and the Senate can be found in publications on rules and the compilations of prior decisions published by each body.

Deschler, Lewis. *Deschler's Precedents of the United States House of Representatives: Including Reference to Provisions of the Constitution and Laws, and to Decisions of the Courts.* U.S. Congress. H. Doc. 94-661. 1977— .

Deschler, Lewis. *Procedure in the United States House of Representatives.* Washington, DC: U.S. Government Printing Office, 1982.
This is a one-volume summary of the ongoing *Deschler's Precedents of the United States House of Representatives: Including Reference to Provisions of the Constitution and Laws, and to Decisions of the Courts.*

Procedure in the U.S. House of Representatives, 1965 Supplement: Annotations of the Precedents of the House for the 97th and 98th Congresses. Prepared by the Office of the Parliamentarian, U.S. House of Representatives. Washington, DC: U.S. Government Printing Office, 1986.

U.S. Congress. House. *Constitution, Jefferson's Manual and the Rules of the House of Representatives.* Washington, DC: U.S. Government Printing Office, 1797— . [Revised biennially]

U.S. Congress. Senate. Committee on Rules and Administration. *Senate Manual Containing the Standing Rules, Orders, Laws, and Resolutions Affecting the Business of the United States Senate*. Washington, DC: U.S. Government Printing Office, 1967— . [Revised biennially]

U.S. Congress. Senate. *Senate Procedure: Precedents and Practices*. Washington, DC: U.S. Government Printing Office, 1981.
This is a one-volume work that arranges precedents of the Senate by subject area.

The clerk of the House of Representatives also issues biennially a pamphlet entitled *Rules of the House of Representatives,* which contains the text of all standing rules of the House. Likewise, the Secretary of the Senate issues the *Standing Rules of the Senate* every two years. These are compilations of each chamber's basic rules with annotations or supplementary material. There is also information on rules on both the Senate Gopher (*gopher:// gopher.senate.gov/*) and the House Gopher (*gopher://gopher.house.gov/*).The World Wide Web home pages for the House (*http://www.house.gov/*) and for the Senate (*http://www.senate.gov/*) offer the same information. In addition, a brief description of the congressional process by Edward F. Willett, entitled *How Our Laws Are Made*, is for sale by the U.S. Government Printing Office and is available on the Internet through the Library of Congress's THOMAS on the World Wide Web and MARVEL on the gopher. It is updated every two years.

Committees

Most of the biographical directories mentioned earlier, including the *CIS/Index*, the *Congressional Staff Directory*, the *Congressional Index*, the *Calendars of the House of Representatives*, the *Official Congressional Directory*, *Politics in America*, and the *Almanac of American Politics*, provide current committee information, such as committee assignments by member and committee rosters. It is important to point out, however, that, while all of these works present information about committee assignments, some offer information about subcommittee membership and some do not. Those that do include subcommittee membership vary in how much information they provide.

Biographical information noting committee assignments can also can be found in the online database services, including CQ'S WASHINGTON ALERT, LEGI-SLATE, LEXIS/NEXIS, and WESTLAW. Information about committee assignments can be found at various sites on the Internet, too. The Library of Congress's MARVEL or either the Senate Gopher or Senate

World Wide Web page or the House Gopher or House World Wide Web page are potential sources. You could also use the Library of Congress's THOMAS on the World Wide Web.

The following reference tools are invaluable for historical purposes.

Nelson, Garrison, ed. *Committees in the U.S. Congress 1947–1992.* 2 vols. Washington, DC: Congressional Quarterly, 1993.
This two-volume set is the most comprehensive reference work on congressional committee membership for the period since 1947. It includes each member's length of membership and leadership positions. The first volume is organized by committee, showing all members assigned for each Congress and members' seniority. The second volume focuses on each member's committee assignments throughout his or her career. This volume also includes descriptions of committee jurisdictions and a history of each committee and the committee system.

Stubbs, Walter, comp. *Congressional Committees 1789–1982: A Checklist.* Westport, CT: Greenwood Press, 1985.
This volume is useful for identifying the more than 1,500 committees that have existed since 1789. It identifies standing, select and special, select and joint special, and statutory joint committees.

Voting Guides

While there are many sources in which one can find roll call votes, including the *Congressional Record*, the *Congressional Index*, and the *Congressional Quarterly Weekly Report*, the online database services, including CQ'S WASHINGTON ALERT, LEXIS/NEXIS, LEGI-SLATE, and WEST-LAW, and through various sites on the Internet, the following two guides are easy to use and very comprehensive.

Busnich, Victor W. *Congressional Voting Guide.* 4th ed. New York: H. W. Wilson, 1992.
This ten-year compilation is divided into two main sections, the House Voting Records and the Senate Voting Records. A brief biography of each member of the 102d Congress, arranged state by state, includes a record of how he or she voted since 1982. Two additional sections, House Measures and Senate Measures, describe every bill and give the date and results of the vote by party. The work also includes a name and subject index.

Congressional Roll Call. Washington, DC: Congressional Quarterly, 1970— .
This annual series began with the first session of the 91st Congress. Each volume opens with an analysis and legislative description of key votes on major issues, followed by special voting
studies, such as freshman voting, bipartisanship, voting participation, and so forth. The remainder of the volume is a member-
by-member analysis, in chronological order, of all roll call votes
in the House and Senate. There is also a roll call subject index. In
the compilation of roll call votes, there is a brief synopsis of each
bill, the total vote, and vote by party affiliation.

Ratings

Over one hundred organizations rate members of Congress on key
votes. Most publish their ratings in their own newsletters or magazines.
The addresses and telephone numbers of these groups and the titles in
which the ratings can be found and their frequency of publication are
listed in a Congressional Research Service report entitled *Organizations
that Rate Members of Congress on Their Voting Record.* The most recent edition of this report was published in 1991. The report is available on microfilm in *Major Studies and Issue Briefs of the Congressional Research Service.*
    Two weekly publications, the *Congressional Quarterly Weekly Report*
and the *National Journal,* publish ratings each year. The *CQ Weekly Report*
began publishing ratings in 1961. It publishes the ratings of four interest
groups as well as the key votes on which these groups evaluated congressional members. Ratings by the same four groups can be found in Congressional Quarterly's directory, *Politics in America.* Only the ratings are given in
this volume, not the key votes on which they are based. Interest group ratings can also be found on CQ's WASHINGTON ALERT online database.
The *National Journal* conducts its own rating, published in the *National Journal* each year since 1982. It analyzes votes in three areas: economic policy,
social affairs, and foreign policy. The *Almanac of American Politics* provides
ratings, though not the key votes, for ten groups. The addresses and telephone numbers of the groups whose ratings are cited are provided in the
front of the *Almanac of American Politics.* Ratings of congressional members
from the *National Journal* and the *Almanac of American Politics* can be found
on LEXIS/NEXIS. The only volume that has collected various ratings over
time is listed below.

Sharp, J. Michael. *Directory of Congressional Voting Scores and Interest Group
Ratings.* 2 vols. New York: Facts on File, 1988.
    This volume provides a comprehensive voting study and group
rating data compilation for every member of Congress since the

beginning of the 80th Congress in 1947. Four categories of ratings scores, all generated by Congressional Quarterly, are included. These are conservative coalition, party unity, presidential support, and voting participation. The volume also presents ratings by eleven groups that represent various areas of concern. The value of this volume is that it provides data back to 1947, when the first ratings were done.

District Data

Congressional Quarterly's *Congressional Districts in the 1990s* (Washington, DC: Congressional Quarterly, 1993) is a political atlas of current congressional districts. This volume includes 1990 census data, state and district profiles, and election results since 1986 recalculated to match the new districts. Earlier information on congressional districts can be found in two similar volumes, CQ's *Congressional Districts in the 1980s* and *Congressional Districts in the 1970s*. Maps and district data are also published by the Census Bureau in its series, *Congressional District Atlas*. This atlas includes maps of the fifty states and the District of Columbia. There are tables that identify the congressional district(s) related to each county and county subdivision, along with a table that identifies the counties that are located entirely or partly in each district.

The following three volumes present population data for both the districts and counties. Along with district and county maps is included information about the creation of the counties. Also provided are the names and party affiliations of representatives for each district by Congress.

Parsons, Stanley B. *United States Congressional Districts, 1883–1913*. New York: Greenwood Press, 1990.

Parsons, Stanley B., William W. Beach, and Dan Herman. *United States Congressional Districts, 1788–1841*. Westport, CT: Greenwood Press, 1978.

Parsons, Stanley B., William W. Beach, and Michael J. Dubin. *United States Congressional Districts, 1843–1883*. New York: Greenwood Press, 1986.

If the kind of data or information you are seeking about a district is of a general nature, two of the almanacs cited earlier, the *Almanac of American Politics* and *Politics in America* can be used as ready reference guides. The three atlases listed earlier in this volume (see page 6) also contain valuable information about congressional districts.

Campaign Finance

The *Congressional Quarterly Weekly Report* and the *National Journal* regularly publish articles on federal campaign finance data. The most recent research guides to campaign spending have been published by Congressional Quarterly.

Makinson, Larry. *Open Secrets: The Encyclopedia of Congressional Money and Politics*. 3d ed. Washington, DC: Congressional Quarterly, 1994.
This edition of *Open Secrets* identifies, classifies, and catalogues the sources and recipients of over $450 million in congressional campaign contributions in the 1992 elections. It analyzes contributions from both PACs and individuals and includes the campaign finance profiles of all 535 members of the 103d Congress. New editions of this work are published every two years.

Morris, Dwight, and Murielle Gamache. *Handbook of Campaign Spending: Money in the 1992 Congressional Races*. Washington, DC: Congressional Quarterly, 1994.
This all new edition of the *Handbook of Campaign Spending* is the second in a series that began with the 1990 elections. This volume uses Federal Election Commission reports and interviews with candidates, staffers, and consultants to present an examination of campaign spending. It also provides a race-by-race analysis of the 1992 House and Senate elections. New editions of this work are published every two years.

The series *Vital Statistics on Congress* also has an excellent section on campaign finance, including information on expenditures and political action committees.

Election Returns

The following guides are the best sources for election returns:

Congressional Quarterly. *Guide to U.S. Elections*. 3d ed. Washington, DC: Congressional Quarterly, 1994.
This work is the most definitive source of statistical data on elections. Included are the complete voting records of elections for the presidency, Congress, and governorships. This volume is an excellent reference guide to all aspects of elections, including extensive background material on the history of parties, preference primaries, demographic data, and redistricting. Accompanying

each major section of the work is a topical bibliography. The format makes this an especially useful reference work. There are three ways by which to locate information. A detailed table of contents provides an overall view of the scope and coverage of the work. There are candidate indexes for presidential, gubernatorial, Senate, and House candidates. Finally, there is a general index, which covers all subjects discussed in the work.

The Election Data Book: A Statistical Portrait of Voting in America. Lanham, MD: Bernan Press, 1993— .
This biennial series presents historical and current statistics on voting results for congressional, senatorial, presidential, and gubernatorial elections. The volume includes more than 150 maps and charts and offers data broken down by state, county, and congressional district on population, race, voting age, registration, turnout, and primary results.

McGillivray, Alice V. *Congressional and Gubernatorial Primaries: 1993–1994: A Handbook of Election Statistics.* Washington, DC: Congressional Quarterly, 1993.
This series, with a new volume to be published every two years, provides the official primary results for members of Congress and governors. Each chapter covers a single state, summarizing the voting data for these offices. Also included are county-by-county tables detailing voter registration and primary voting.

Scammon, Richard M., and Alice V. McGillivray, comps. *America Votes: A Handbook of Contemporary American Election Statistics.*Washington, DC: Congressional Quarterly, 1955— .
This biennial work presents presidential, congressional, and gubernatorial returns. It also includes data for primary elections. The total vote (Republican and Democratic), pluralities, and percentages per county and congressional district are reported. Sections on each of the states include the following: a map of the state depicting counties and congressional districts; a geographical breakdown by county for presidential, senatorial, and gubernatorial returns; and tables of the congressional returns by district.

The *National Journal* and the *Congressional Quarterly Weekly Report* also publish the results of the elections in a special issue a week following an election. For a week-by-week analysis of a campaign and election, these two journals, as well as *The New York Times* and the *Washington Post*, are indispensable. Also, the online database services and various sites on the Internet contain data on campaign contributions and spending and primary and election statistics. These are invaluable for following an election campaign on a day-to-day basis.

Congressional Support Agencies

The four support agencies of Congress—the Congressional Research Service, the Congressional Budget Office, the Office of Technology Assessment, and the General Accounting Office—publish a variety of reports and studies useful for researching legislation and Congress itself. Many of these publications are listed in the *Monthly Catalog* and on the various CD-ROM indexes to government documents (Government Documents Catalog Subscription Service, GPO on Silver Platter, and Government Publications Index on InfoTrac). Some publications and the testimony of officials from all four agencies are indexed in *CIS Index*. At the end of the description of each agency that follows we list additional tools that can be used to identify the publications of that agency. Finally, all four agencies submit an annual report to Congress that details their activities and plans.

Congressional Research Service

The Library of Congress was established in 1800 as a congressional resource. While it maintains a special relationship to Congress, its function as a congressional resource is primarily in conjunction with the Congressional Research Service (CRS). The CRS works exclusively for members of Congress and congressional committees. Most CRS reports can only be obtained through a representative, senator, or committee office. Sometimes a report will be published by a congressional committee in the form of a committee print. The CRS publishes the *Digest of Public General Bills and Resolutions*. Available by subscription from the U.S. Government Printing Office, the *Digest* summarizes all legislation introduced in each session of Congress. It identifies the sponsor and co-sponsor of the legislation, lists identical bills, notes its short title, offers a subject index, and provides a brief factual description. The *Digest* is printed in five cumulative issues each year, supplemented by biweekly updates.

Publications of the CRS are available on microfilm in the series *Major Studies of the Legislative Reference Service/Congressional Research Service: 1916–1974* and yearly its supplements, *Major Studies and Issue Briefs of the Congressional Research Service*. The original collection and each supplement comes with a printed guide providing a title/author guide and subject index. These sets cover such areas as legal and constitutional issues, the

Congress, government and political issues, and foreign and defense issues. University Publications of America, which publishes the series, has also published a two-volume cumulative index for the years 1916 to 1989. The first volume of this index contains a bibliography and supplementary indexes; the second volume contains an index organized by subjects and names. University Publications of America has also published the index on CD-ROM. The Congressional Research Service Index on CD-ROM has annual editions as well as a retrospective edition covering 1916 to 1993. The annual edition for 1994 will be published in 1995. This CD-ROM product indexes over 8,500 CRS reports by subject, author, title, CRS document number, and issuing division.

The CRS has published a number of bibliographies on Congress, which are updated irregularly. All of these cover the same areas, including history, procedure, reorganization and reform, party leadership, committee system, staff and support agencies, roll call analysis, and policy studies. They are available on microfilm in the *Major Studies and Issue Briefs of the Congressional Research Service*. Since 1980, CRS has also published a journal, *CRS Review*. Aimed at individuals interested in congressional affairs, it focuses on public policy issues. Another useful tool is the CRS journal *Major Legislation of the Congress*. It provides summaries of congressional issues and major legislation. Each issue is cumulative, and the final issue, published at the end of each Congress, can be used as a permanent reference tool.

Congressional Budget Office

To implement the new budget procedures established by the Budget Act of 1974, Congress created three new institutions, one of which was the newest of the congressional support agencies, the Congressional Budget Office (CBO). The CBO was established as the legislative branch's counterpart to the executive branch's Office of Management and Budget. The CBO is a nonpartisan organization that provides Congress with economic forecasts and fiscal policy analyses. Its objective is to present Congress with different public policy options and their budgetary impact. It also develops cost estimates for carrying out legislation reported by committees. These projections find their way into committee reports and often into floor debate on a bill.

The CBO publishes a *List of Publications*, which is cumulative. The *List of Publications* is arranged both chronologically and by subject. Topics covered include the economy and fiscal policy, the federal budget, commerce, trade and industry, social programs, national security, and government operations.

Office of Technology Assessment

The Office of Technology Assessment (OTA) was established in 1973 and abolished in 1995. The OTA conducted a number of assessments in such areas as energy, food, health, transportation, oceans, and materials resources. The OTA relied to a large extent on teams of specialists assembled from government, academia, and industry to prepare its assessments. Requests for assessments originated with the chair of a congressional committee, a congressional member of the OTA board, or with the OTA's director. The OTA's *List of Publications* provided annotated listings of publications by broad subject areas, including energy, industry, technology, employment, international security and commerce, biological applications, food and renewable resources, health, communication and information technology, oceans and the environment, science, education, and transportation. These research reports are excellent materials for anyone doing research on legislation relating to those topics.

General Accounting Office

The General Accounting Office (GAO) is the largest and second oldest of the congressional support agencies. The GAO was established by the Budget and Accounting Act of 1921 to audit spending by federal departments and agencies. Often referred to as the watchdog of Congress, the GAO was created in part to assist Congress in fulfilling its oversight responsibilities. You should always check to see whether the GAO has published a report on the particular area of government operations you are researching. The *GAO Journal*, published quarterly, sometimes contains articles on the activities of the GAO and Congress. The agency is engaged in monitoring federal spending to ensure that programs are being implemented efficiently and in accordance with legislative intent. The Legislative Reorganization Acts of 1946 and 1970 and the Congressional Budget and Impoundment Control Act have charged the GAO with investigative responsibilities as well. It provides Congress with numerous audits and studies requested by congressional committees and members of Congress, studies directed by statute, testimony at congressional hearings, and commentary on new legislation. The GAO publishes an extensive series of reports on the operations of various government programs. A two-volume publication, *Abstracts of Reports and Testimony* and *Indexes for Reports and Testimony*, is published yearly. The first volume contains full abstracts of reports and testimony; the second volume has several indexes to help identify a particular report or testimony by subject, issue, title, or GAO witness. The U.S. Government Printing Office also publishes a monthly equivalent entitled *Reports and Testimony*. GAO reports and other publications are available on the Internet via Wiretap at *gopher://*

wiretap.Spies.com or via the World Wide Web at *http://wiretap.Spies.com*. These provide the full text of reports. They are also available via GPO ACCESS.

Informal Congressional Groups

In addition to formal groups, there are numerous informal congressional groups. Generally, informal groups, some bipartisan, form around common issues, interests, or geographic concerns and membership is optional though a membership fee may be required. They have increased in number since the late 1970s. The best access to materials published by congressional groups is the new CIS guide and microfiche collection, *Congressional Member Organizations and Caucuses: Publications and Policy Materials*. The first annual guide and companion microfiche collection of this set were published in 1992 and cover publications issued during 1991. The index provides access by subject, name, institution, bill and act names, and bill numbers. Starting in late 1995 the *Congressional Member Organizations and Caucuses* will be available on Congressional Masterfile II.

C-SPAN

The Cable Satellite Public Affairs Network (C-SPAN) is one of the most important developments for students of Congress. This live broadcast of congressional proceedings, begun in 1979, provides gavel-to-gavel coverage of the House and Senate, plus other public affairs programming such as National Press Club speeches, policy addresses, debates, and public policy forums and call-in programs. C-SPAN broadcasts on two 24–hour channels: C-SPAN I, which carries the House, and C-SPAN II, which airs the Senate. For anyone researching Congress or a specific piece of legislation, C-SPAN helps make the process come alive. C-SPAN publishes a *U.S. Congress Handbook*, which is a handy reference tool to members of Congress and contains a special section with information about C-SPAN and many of the organizations that are a part of the network's coverage. The C-SPAN Gopher's World Wide Web menu includes information about programs, press releases, voting data, and how to send e-mail to C-SPAN. The C-SPAN Gopher address is *gopher:///C-span.org/* and the World Wide Web address is *http://www.C-span.org*.

The Public Affairs Video Archives, located at Purdue University, has recorded, cataloged, indexed and distributed all programming on both channels of C-SPAN since October 1987. The Archives has also published a CD-ROM product entitled Public Affairs Chronicle. The first issue covers 1991. The Public Affairs Chronicle is a database of over 12,500 primary source public affairs events that covers C-SPAN as well as events not covered by C-SPAN. It includes over 8,700 full text transcripts that can be searched and read. A CD-ROM covering 1992 is in progress, and plans are underway for more recent years. This new CD-ROM product is the best way to search all the events covered by C-SPAN. The facility is open to the public. For information about other services and programs contact the Archives directly.

Oral Histories

Oral histories are an excellent primary resource for research on Congress. The following are two oral history collections that focus on Congress.

United States Senate Historical Office Oral History Collection: Interviews with Senate Staff. Wilmington, DE: Scholarly Resources, 1984— .
These interviews with retired Senate staff members provide insights into Senate personalities and Senate operations. Twenty-four oral histories have been completed. These interviews, plus an index, are available on microfiche.

Former Members of Congress Oral History Collection. Sanford, NC: Microfilming Corporation of America, 1981.
This collection of seventy-nine oral histories by both senators and representatives covers the period from 1922 to 1977.

Audiovisual Materials

Video cassettes can often provide a better understanding of how Congress works through their ability to show the legislative process in action. *We the People*, a series of twenty-six half-hour cassettes, presents the day-to-day activities of Congress, with analysis and commentary by political scientists. Among some of the topics covered are congressional elections, committee leadership, lobbying, constituent relations, lawmaking, budgeting, ethics, the courts, and relations with the president and the media. The series was produced by the American Political Science Association and WETA, a public television station in Washington, D.C. The American Political Science Association has published both a study guide and faculty guide to accompany the series.

An excellent 90–minute documentary entitled "The Congress," coauthored and narrated by David McCullough, is available from Direct Cinema Limited. This videorecording was directed by the award-winning filmmaker Ken Burns. The four-part series, *The Power Game*, written and narrated by the journalist and reporter Hedrick Smith, includes one part entitled "The Congress." This is available from PBS. Another good video cassette is "An Act of Congress," produced by the Learning Corporation of America. Boston's public television station, WGBH, and Harvard University have produced a set of fifteen half-hour video cassettes on American government including three video cassettes about Congress—"The Functions of Congress," "Congressional Reform," and "Congress and the President." Video Insight distributes several half-hour video cassettes, including "A Day in the Life of Congress," "How a Bill Becomes a Law," "The Legislative Process," and "The President and Congress."

Audio cassettes are another source of information. National Public Radio sells a wide variety of cassettes that relate to Congress on topics such as women politicians, campaigning, elections, and National Press Club speeches. Many libraries collect video and audio cassettes, so be sure to check on what is available.

Internet Sources

The Internet is a worldwide computer network, that is accessible to a wide variety of users, including individuals, schools, libraries, universities, businesses, and many other groups and organizations around the world. Internet users have access to software programs, library catalogs, databases, documents, electronic mail, images and sound, and electronic discussion groups. Perhaps the best way to introduce yourself to the Internet is to use one of the many books that describe how it works and what it includes. New books on the Internet are being published regularly, but some of the better known are *The Internet Directory, The Whole Internet: Users' Guide and Catalog, The Internet Complete Reference*, and the *World Wide Web Unleashed.*

Internet users can access all kinds of federal government information, including Supreme Court decisions, census data, White House briefings, committee assignments, congressional directories and biographies, legislation, abstracts of Congressional Research Service reports, testimony and reports issued by the General Accounting Office, bibliographies of Senate hearings, prints and publications, and congressional e-mail addresses. This is just a sample of what is available on the Internet, which expands daily.

Some of the sources already mentioned, as well as many others, are described in *Internet Sources of Government Information* (2d ed., February 26, 1994) by Blake Gumprecht. Current and future editions of this work can be retrieved through anonymous FTP and e-mail, and via Gopher from the University of Michigan's Clearinghouse of Subject-Oriented Internet Resource Guides at *gopher://una.hh.lib.umich.edu* or via the World Wide Web at *http://www.lib.umich.edu/chouse.* Once there, go into the "inetdirs" folder, followed by the "guides on the social sciences" folder. This second edition of *Internet Sources of Government Information* includes more than 325 sources of information and provides both Gopher sources and Telnet addresses when known. The preferred source is often a Gopher source because of the ease of the software.

Bruce Maxwell's book *How to Access the Federal Government on the Internet: Washington Online* (Washington, DC: Congressional Quarterly, 1995) is another helpful guide to Internet resources. He provides detailed descriptions of more than 250 Internet sites and discusses how to access the text of bills, lists of holdings at the National Archives, and electronic sources at the Library of Congress. The *Federal Internet Source*, published by National Journal and the Internet Letter in 1995, contains up-to-date descriptions, listings, addresses, and home pages of more than 500 federal, state, and other political Internet sites.

The Library of Congress' MARVEL offers a variety of government and congressional information and is accessible via Gopher at *marvel.loc.gov* and via the Library of Congress's home page at *http://www.loc.gov* on the World Wide Web. MARVEL includes the full text of the *Congressional Record* (starting with the 103d Congress) and information about floor proceedings and amendments, and access to the *United States Code*, bills, and committee action via GPO ACCESS. The GPO ACCESS database includes the *Congressional Record* (starting with 1994), the *History of Bills* (starting with 1994), the *United States Code* (starting with 1994), *Congressional Bills* (starting with the 103d Congress), the *Federal Register* (starting with 1994), and numerous other databases.

The Library of Congress has activated a new electronic tool, dubbed THOMAS, that provides users with access to government information over the World Wide Web on the Internet. THOMAS gathers several government resources into one place. It contains the full text of legislation, the full text of the *Congressional Record*, Senate and House information, and C-SPAN. THOMAS supplements much of the same online information found in the Library of Congress's MARVEL system, but THOMAS offers hypertext links as well. THOMAS is accessible on the World Wide Web: *http://thomas.loc.gov*. Another World Wide Web site is CapWeb: A Guide to the US Congress (*http://policy.net/capweb*). It provides biographical information on members of Congress and pointers to other sources of information. Another World Wide Web site is Politics USA (*http://politicsusa.com*). It was created by National Journal and the American Political Network. It includes up-to-the-minute news from Congress, the White House, and campaigns. You can also search recent legislation by keyword on CapWeb. Many individual members of Congress now have home pages on the World Wide Web.

There are several Gophers that are of interest to the researcher of Congress. For example, there is the C-SPAN Gopher, whose menu includes information about programs, press releases, voting data, and how to send e-mail to C-SPAN. It can be reached at *gopher://C-span.org/*. C-SPAN now has its own home page on the World Wide Web. Web browsers will find the C-SPAN home page at *http://www.C-span.org*. Congressional Quarterly has a new CQ Gopher which is offered free of charge to Internet users. Lead stories of the current *Congressional Quarterly Weekly Report*, articles from its special reports, weekly news briefs from *CQ Researcher*, the statuses of appropriations bills and other major legislation from CQ'S WASHINGTON ALERT, the results of key roll call votes, updates on congressional and gubernatorial elections, and information on members of Congress all can be found in CQ Gopher. To access, Internet users should point their gopher at *gopher://gopher.cqalert.com/*. There is also a Gopher for the House (*gopher://gopher.house.gov/*) and a Gopher for the Senate (*gopher://gopher.senate.gov/*).

Another useful book is *How to Access the Government's Electronic Bulletin Boards: Washington Online* (Washington, DC: Congressional Quarterly, 1994) by Bruce Maxwell. This book provides explanations of how to log on to each federal bulletin board and how to use it, and gives detailed descriptions of what each board offers. A sampling of some of the information available through free federal bulletin boards includes lists of contacts at federal agencies; government statistics on income, poverty, population growth, immigration, taxes, government revenue, and school financing; and transcripts of President Clinton's speeches. Most of the bulletin boards have menu systems that make it easy for inexperienced computer users to find the information they seek. Maxwell shows how to navigate the menu and how to download the bulletin board information. As you work, keep in mind that the Internet system is continually in flux. System addresses, source directories, and file names change. Some items disappear altogether and other remote systems may be unavailable, so patience and perseverance are required.

Archives

Archives contain original documents such as letters, memos, reports, and other forms of primary research material. There are several guides that can help you locate relevant archival material.

Miller, Cynthia P. *Guide to the Research Collections of Former Members of the U.S. House of Representatives, 1789–1989*. Washington, DC: U.S. Government Printing Office, 1988.

Jacob, Kathryn A., ed. *Guide to Research Collections of Former United States Senators, 1789–1982*. Detroit: Gale, 1986.

McDonough, John J., comp. *Members of Congress: A Checklist of Their Papers in the Manuscript Division, Library of Congress*. Washington, DC: Library of Congress, 1980.

National Archives and Records Administration. *Guide to the Records of the United States House of Representatives at the National Archives, 1789–1989*. Washington, DC: U.S. Government Printing Office, 1989.

National Archives and Records Administration. *Guide to the Records of the United States Senate at the National Archives, 1789–1989*. Washington, DC: U.S. Government Printing Office, 1989.

Data Archives

The major social science data archive is the Inter-University Consortium for Political and Social Research at the University of Michigan. For more information about the archive's holdings, you should consult the consortium's most recent *Guide to Resources and Services*. This publication also includes information about training programs, classes, remote access computer assistance, and information on how to obtain data and codebooks. Its listing of archival holdings provides the name of the data collector, the title and detailed description of the data file, and related publications that have used the data. For example, amongst the numerous data files related to Congress, you can find information on roll call voting records, voting scores, biographical data, election returns, district data, and public opinion polls.

Case Law

Supreme Court decisions, first issued as "slip opinions" that are available within three days in depository libraries, are published in the five current reports listed below. A useful introductory guide to the judicial process and how opinions are written can be found in Tyll R. van Geel's *Understanding Supreme Court Opinions* (New York: Longman, 1991).

U.S. Law Week. Washington, DC: Bureau of National Affairs, 1933— .
This weekly periodical service includes important sections on the Supreme Court. It has four indexes: a topical index, a table of cases, a docket number table, and a proceedings section. In addition to containing the full text of all decisions, the periodical includes information on new statutes and agency rulings. The most valuable feature of this tool is its rapid publication of Supreme Court decisions.

United States Supreme Court Bulletin. Washington, DC: Commerce Clearing House, 1936— .

This looseleaf service contains current Supreme Court decisions and a docket of Supreme Court cases. It is especially useful for research on the current Court.

U.S. Supreme Court. *Supreme Court Reporter*. St. Paul, MN: West Publishing Company, 1983— .
This weekly nongovernmental publication contains annotated reports and indexes of case names. It includes opinions of justices in chambers.

U.S. Supreme Court. *United States Reports*. Washington, DC: U.S. Government Printing Office, 1790— .
This annual publication of the official text of all opinions of the Supreme Court also includes a table of cases reported, a table of cases and statutes cited, miscellaneous materials, and a subject index. All written reports and most *per curiam* reports of decisions are printed. Beginning with the 1970 term, chamber opinions are included.

U.S. Supreme Court. *United States Supreme Court Reports: Lawyers' Edition*. Rochester, NY: Lawyers Co-Operative Publishing Company, 1970— .
This annual service publishes all Supreme Court cases. It contains numerous *per curiam* decisions not found elsewhere and individually summarizes the majority and dissenting opinions and counsel briefs. The index to annotations leads to the legal notes provided for each case.

Digests of Supreme Court Decisions

The following are excellent finding tools that identify digests of Supreme Court decisions by subject and case name.

Digest of United States Supreme Court Reports, Annotated with Case Annotations, Dissenting and Separate Decisions since 1900. Rochester, NY: Lawyers Co-Operative Publishing Company, 1948— .

United States Supreme Court Digest. St. Paul, MN: West Publishing Company, 1940— .

Shepard's United States Citations is also helpful in that it identifies instances where a decision has been cited in a later case, allowing the searcher to follow changes in legal interpretation.

Briefs and Records of the Supreme Court

Briefs and oral arguments used by counsel records are a valuable resource for understanding the eventual decision of a case and the interpretation of a statute or administrative rule. Many libraries have these records available on microfiche. The Congressional Information Service publishes two series on microfiche—the *U.S. Supreme Court Records and Briefs* and *Oral Arguments of the U.S. Supreme Court*. The database LEXIS/NEXIS contains briefs beginning with 1979. Other sources for briefs and arguments follow.

Kurland, Philip B., and Gerhard Casper. *Landmark Briefs and Arguments of the Supreme Court of the United States: Constitutional Law*. Frederick, MD: University Publications of America, 1975— .
This series covers hundreds of constitutional cases since 1793. The series includes facsimile reproductions of briefs as they were originally filed at the Supreme Court and transcripts of oral arguments as provided by the Supreme Court Library. Beginning with the volumes for the 1989–1990 term, the series contains the text of all Supreme Court decisions.

U.S. National Archives and Records Service. *Tape Recordings of Oral Arguments before the U.S. Supreme Court*. Washington, DC: National Archives and Records Service, 1955— .
Tapes are available for purchase only after three years have elapsed.

Administrative Law

The *Federal Register* and the *Code of Federal Regulations* contain a current compilation of all rules and regulations issued by executive departments and agencies. The *Federal Register*, which is issued daily, contains presidential documents, rules and regulations, proposed rules and notices to the public of proposed rules, notices and other documents other than rules that are of interest to the public, and notices of meetings. In effect, it serves as a daily update of the *Code of Federal Regulations*. When an agency adopts a new rule, it is published in the *Federal Register*. When the *Code of Federal Regulations* is updated, all of these rules are inserted into the appropriate part of the *Code of Federal Regulations*.

Every issue of the *Federal Register* includes a number of bibliographic tools. These "finding aids," help the researcher locate a variety of specific information. The "Contents" section contains a complete listing of all proposed and final rules, as well as notices, arranged by agency. Each entry includes the beginning page number of the document and a brief description. The "Notices" section is arranged by agency name and provides the dates of scheduled meetings. The *"Code of Federal Regulations* Parts Affected in This Issue" section provides a listing of titles and parts of the *Code of Federal Regulations* that have been, or will be, affected by rules contained within that day's issue. An allied section lists these changes cumulatively for the month. The "Reader Aids" section assists the user in finding specific information. The *"Federal Register* Pages and Dates" section is a table showing which inclusive pages correspond to which dates for the current month's *Federal Register.* Finally, the "Information and Assistance" section provides a listing of Office of Federal Register telephone numbers to call for help with detailed questions.

An important finding aid is the *Federal Register Index,* published separately from the *Federal Register.* Published monthly and annually, this index is arranged by agency and provides citations to all proposed and final rules and notices that have been printed in the *Federal Register* for the last quarter or year.

The *Code of Federal Regulations* is a codification of the rules published in the *Federal Register* by all of the executive departments and agencies. It is arranged into fifty titles that represent broad subject areas. Each title contains regulations pertaining to a single subject area and consists of one or more chapters. Each chapter presents a single agency's regulations. The chapters are further divided into parts, and the parts into sections. If necessary, sections are broken down into paragraphs. As most titles cover a broad area, regulations are typically contained in more than one book. However, all of a particular agency's regulations are located in a single title. Every volume of the *Code* includes a "Table of *CFR* Titles and Chapters," which lists the subject areas of the regulations contained in each title and the name of the agency for the corresponding chapter. Following the codified material, each volume offers several finding aids. Also included is an alphabetical list of the agencies whose regulations appear in the *Code* and a citation to the title and chapter where they are located. In addition, all changes made by documents published in the *Federal Register* are enumerated in a "List of *CFR* Sections Affected." Every three months, one-quarter of the *Code* is revised and reissued. By the end of each year it has been completely revised. The revision date is printed on the cover of each volume.

The *CFR Index,* revised annually, is a separate volume of the *Code of Federal Regulations* that consists of an index arranged by agency name and by subject heading. Citations include the title and parts of the *Code* where the rules pertaining to a subject or agency can be found. Also included in the *Index* are agency-prepared indexes for each volume of the *Code,* a "Parallel Table of Statutory Authorities and Rules," a "List of *CFR*

Titles, Chapters, Subchapters, and Parts," and an "Alphabetical Listing of Agencies," appearing in the *Code*.

Finally, the *LSA—List of CFR Sections Affected*, published monthly, is a cumulative update to the *Code of Federal Regulations*. The starting date for each title in the *LSA* is the date when the *Code* volume containing that title was last revised. The *LSA* is intended to assist users of the *Code* in finding amendments published in the *Federal Register*. The entries are arranged by *Code* title, chapter, part, and section and denote the change made. The *LSA* also contains a "Checklist of Current *CFR* Volumes" for the month, a "Parallel Table of Authorities and Rules," and a "Table of *Federal Register* Issue Pages and Dates." Instead of going through numerous issues of the *Federal Register* to find out what new rules, amendments, or proposed rules have been promulgated since the *CFR* was last updated, it is best to use this source.

Finding Tools

While the *Federal Register* and *Code Federal Regulations* are the primary source and finding tools relating to rules and regulations, other indexes are available to aid in finding administrative citations. The full text of the *Federal Register* is available on the Internet through GPO ACCESS, starting with 1994. There is also a CD-ROM product entitled CD/FR: Compact Disk Federal Register, first published in 1993. These two tools, as well as the two listed below, are perhaps easier to use than the *Federal Register* and *Code of Federal Regulations* themselves.

CIS Federal Register Index. Bethesda, MD: Congressional Information Service, 1984— .

This weekly index contains four parts. An index by subject and name provides access by subjects, geographical areas, issuing agency, industries, corporations, organizations, individual names, and legislation. There is a calendar of effective dates and comment deadlines. The index by *CFR* section numbers specifies when and where final or proposed changes to the *CFR* have been announced. Finally, there is an index by agency docket numbers. Each index entry provides the issuing agency, register issue date, type of document, and *Federal Register* page number.

Index to the Code of Federal Regulations. Bethesda, MD: Congressional Information Service, 1977— .

This annual service has a detailed subject index that allows a search of all fifty titles at once. You can search a general or specific subject and be referred to all relevant parts and subparts.

There are two geographical indexes. The first indexes regulations regarding political jurisdictions, such as states, countries, and cities. The second cites properties administered by the federal government, such as parks and military bases. There also are two additional indexes that can save time if you already have a citation. A list of descriptive headings gives headings assigned to each part of the *CFR;* a list of reserved headings indicates which parts of the *CFR* have been designated reserved, either for future use or because they have been vacated from use. Starting with 1991, there are also quarterly updates and an index by *CFR* section numbers.

Selected Bibliography
on Congress

History and Development of Congress

Bailey, Stephen K., and Howard D. Samuel. *Congress at Work*. New York: Holt, 1952.

Baker, Ross K. *House and Senate*. 2d ed. New York: W.W. Norton, 1995.

Barber, Sotirios A. *The Constitution and the Delegation of Congressional Power*. Chicago: University of Chicago Press, 1975.

Bates, Ernest S. *The Story of Congress 1789–1935*. New York: Harper, 1936.

Berman, Daniel M. *In Congress Assembled: The Legislative Process in the National Government*. New York: Macmillan, 1964.

Bibby, John F., and Roger H. Davidson. *Studies in the Legislative Process on Capitol Hill*. 2d ed. Hinsdale, IL: Dryden, 1972.

Bowling, Kenneth R. *Politics in the First Congress, 1789–1791*. New York: Garland Publishing, 1990.

Boykin, Edward C. *Congress and the Civil War*. New York: McBride, 1955.

Brenner, Philip. *The Limits and Possibilities of Congress*. New York: St. Martin's Press, 1983.

Brock, William R. *An American Crisis: Congress and the Reconstruction, 1865–1867*. New York: St. Martin's Press, 1963.

Burnett, Edmund C. *The Continental Congress*. New York: W.W. Norton, 1941.

Burnham, James. *Congress and the American Tradition*. Chicago: Regnery, 1959.

Clapp, Charles L. *The Congressman: His Work as He Sees It*. Washington, DC: Brookings Institution, 1963.

Clark, Joseph S. *Congress: The Sapless Branch*. New York: Harper and Row, 1964.

Congressional Quarterly. *How Congress Works*. 2d ed. Washington, DC: Congressional Quarterly, 1991.

————. *Origins and Development of Congress*. Washington, DC: Congressional Quarterly, 1976.

————. *Powers of Congress*. Washington, DC: Congressional Quarterly, 1976.

Cummings, Frank. *Capitol Hill Manual*. 2d ed. Washington, DC: Bureau of National Affairs, 1984.

Davidson, Roger H. *The Role of the Congressmen*. New York: Pegasus, 1969.

Davidson, Roger H., and Walter J. Oleszek. *Congress against Itself*. Bloomington: Indiana University Press, 1979.

————. *Congress and Its Members*. 4th ed. Washington, DC: CQ Press, 1993.

Deering, Christopher J., ed. *Congressional Politics*. Chicago: Dorsey Press, 1989.

De Grazia, Alfred, ed. *Congress: The First Branch of Government*. Garden City, NY: Doubleday Anchor Books, 1967.

Dexter, Lewis A. *The Sociology and Politics of Congress*. Chicago: Rand McNally, 1969.

Dodd, Lawrence C. *Congress and Public Policy*. Morristown, NJ: General Learning Press, 1975.

Dodd, Lawrence C., and Bruce I. Oppenheimer, eds. *Congress Reconsidered.* 2d ed. Washington, DC: CQ Press, 1981.

——, eds. *Congress Reconsidered.* 3d ed. Washington, DC: CQ Press, 1985.

——, eds. *Congress Reconsidered.* 4th ed. Washington, DC: CQ Press, 1989.

——, eds. *Congress Reconsidered.* 5th ed. Washington, DC: CQ Press, 1993.

Dodd, Lawrence C., and Richard L. Schott. *Congress and the Administrative State.* New York: Wiley, 1979.

Fiorina, Morris P. *Congress: Keystone of the Washington Establishment.* 2d ed. New Haven, CT: Yale University Press, 1989.

Fisher, Louis. *Constitutional Conflicts between Congress and the President.* Princeton, NJ: Princeton University Press, 1985.

Galloway, George B. *Congress at the Crossroads with Analysis of Operation of Legislative Reorganization Act.* New York: Crowell, 1953.

Groennings, Sven, and Jonathan P. Hawley, eds. *To Be a Congressman: The Promise and the Power.* Washington, DC: Acropolis Books, 1973.

Harris, Joseph P. *Congress and the Legislative Process.* 2d ed. New York: McGraw-Hill, 1972.

Henderson, H. James. *Party Politics in the Continental Congress.* New York: McGraw-Hill, 1974.

Hertzke, Allen D., and Ronald M. Peters, Jr., eds. *The Atomistic Congress: An Interpretation of Congressional Change.* Armonk, NY: M.E. Sharpe, 1992.

Hinckley, Barbara. *Stability and Change in Congress.* 4th ed. New York: Harper and Row, 1988.

Huitt, Ralph K., and Robert L. Peabody. *Congress: Two Decades of Analysis.* New York: Harper and Row, 1969.

Jewell, Malcolm E., and Samuel C. Patterson. *The Legislative Process in the United States*. 4th ed. New York: Random House, 1986.

Jillson, Calvin, and Rick K. Wilson. *Congressional Dynamics: Structure, Coordination, & Choice in the First American Congress, 1774–1789*. Stanford, CA: Stanford University Press, 1994.

Jones, Charles O. *The United States Congress: People, Place, and Policy*. Homewood, IL: Dorsey Press, 1982.

Josephy, Alvin M. *On the Hill: A History of the American Congress from 1789 to the Present*. New York: Simon and Schuster, 1979.

Keefe, William J. *Congress and the American People*. 3d ed. Englewood Cliffs, NJ: Prentice-Hall, 1988.

Keefe, William J., and Morris S. Ogul. *The American Legislative Process: Congress and the States*. 8th ed. Englewood Cliffs, NJ: Prentice-Hall, 1993.

Kolodziej, Edward A. *The Uncommon Defense and Congress, 1945–1963*. Columbus: Ohio State University Press, 1966.

Kornberg, Allan. *Legislatures in Comparative Perspective*. New York: McKay, 1973.

Krehbiel, Keith W. *Information and Legislative Organization*. Ann Arbor: University of Michigan Press, 1991.

Lees, John D., and Malcolm Shaw. *Committees in Legislatures: A Comparative Analysis*. Durham, NC: Duke University Press, 1979.

Livermore, Seward W. *Politics Is Adjourned: Woodrow Wilson and the War Congress, 1916–1918*. Middletown, CT: Wesleyan University Press, 1966.

Loewenberg, Gerhard, and Samuel C. Patterson. *Comparing Legislatures*. Boston: Little, Brown, 1979.

Luce, Robert. *Congress: An Explanation*. Cambridge, MA: Harvard University Press, 1926.

Mann, Thomas E., and Norman J. Ornstein, eds. *The New Congress*. Washington, DC: American Enterprise Institute for Public Policy Research, 1981.

Matthews, Donald R. *U.S. Senators and Their World*. Chapel Hill: University of North Carolina Press, 1960.

McCubbins, Mathew D., and Terry O. Sullivan, eds. *Congress: Structure and Policy*. New York: Cambridge University Press, 1987.

Mezey, Michael L. *Comparative Legislatures*. Durham, NC: Duke University Press, 1979.

Morgan, Donald G. *Congress and the Constitution: A Study of Responsibility*. Cambridge, MA: Harvard University Press, 1966.

Orfield, Gary. *Congressional Power: Congress and Social Change*. New York: Harcourt Brace Jovanovich, 1975.

Ornstein, Norman J., ed. *Congress in Change: Evolution and Change*. New York: Praeger, 1975.

Parker, Glenn R., ed. *Studies of Congress*. Washington, DC: CQ Press, 1985.

Patterson, James T. *Congressional Conservatism and the New Deal*. Lexington: University Press of Kentucky, 1967.

Porter, David L. *Congress and the Waning of the New Deal*. Washington, NY: Kennikat Press, 1980.

Rakove, Jack N. *The Beginnings of National Politics: An Interpretive History of the Continental Congress*. New York: Knopf, 1979.

Reid, T. R. *Congressional Odyssey: The Saga of a Senate Bill*. San Francisco: W.H. Freeman, 1980.

Rieselbach, Leroy N. *Congressional Politics: The Evolving Legislative System*. Boulder, CO: Westview Press, 1995.

——. *The Congressional System: Notes and Readings*. 2d ed. North Scituate, MA: Duxbury Press, 1979.

Ripley, Randall B. *Congress: Process and Policy*. 4th ed. New York: W.W. Norton, 1988.

——. *Kennedy and the Congress*. Morristown, NJ: General Learning Press, 1972.

Ripley, Randall B., and Grace A. Franklin. *Congress, the Bureaucracy, and Public Policy.* 5th ed. Pacific Grove, CA: Brooks/Cole Publishing, 1991.

Robinson, William H., and Clay H. Wellborn. *Knowledge, Power and the Congress.* Washington, DC: Congressional Quarterly, 1991.

Saloma, John S. *Congress and the New Politics.* Boston: Little, Brown, 1969.

Schneier, Edward V., and Bertram Gross. *Congress Today.* New York: St. Martin's Press, 1993.

———. *Legislative Strategy: Shaping Public Policy.* New York: St. Martin's Press, 1993.

Schwab, Larry M. *Changing Patterns of Congressional Politics.* New York: Van Nostrand, 1980.

Schwarz, John E., and L. Earl Shaw. *The United States Congress in Comparative Perspective.* Hinsdale, IL: Dryden, 1976.

Shepsle, Kenneth A., and Barry R. Weingast, eds. *Positive Theories of Congressional Institutions.* Ann Arbor: University of Michigan Press, 1995.

Sundquist, James L. *The Decline and Resurgence of Congress.* Washington, DC: Brookings Institution, 1981.

Tacheron, Donald G., and Morris K. Udall. *The Job of the Congressman: An Introduction to Service in the U.S. House of Representatives.* 2d ed. Indianapolis: Bobbs–Merrill, 1970.

Thomas, Norman C., and Karl A. Lamb. *Congress: Politics and Practice.* New York: Random House, 1964.

Thompson, Margaret S. *The 'Spider Web': Congress and Lobbying in the Age of Grant.* Ithaca, NY: Cornell University Press, 1985.

Truman, David B., ed. *The Congress and America's Future.* Englewood Cliffs, NJ: Prentice-Hall, 1973.

Uslaner, Eric M. *The Decline of Comity in Congress.* Ann Arbor: University of Michigan Press, 1993.

Vogler, David J. *The Politics of Congress*. 6th ed. Madison, WI: WCB Brown and Benchmark, 1993.

Wachtel, Ted. *The Electronic Congress: A Blueprint for Participatory Democracy*. Pipersville, PA: Piper's Press, 1992.

Wilson, Woodrow. *Congressional Government*. Boston: Houghton Mifflin, 1885.

Wright, Gerald C., Jr., Leroy N. Rieselbach, and Lawrence C. Dodd, eds. *Congress and Policy Change*. New York: Agathon Press, 1986.

Young, James S. *The Washington Community, 1800–1829*. New York: Columbia University Press, 1966.

Young, Roland A. *The American Congress*. New York: Harper and Row, 1958.

Congressional Process

Alexander, DeAlva S. *History and Procedure of the House of Representatives*. Boston: Houghton Mifflin, 1916.

Bach, Stanley, and Steven S. Smith. *Managing Uncertainty in the House of Representatives: Adaptation and Innovation in Special Rules*. Washington, DC: Brookings Institution, 1988.

Bailey, Christopher J. *The Republican Party in the U.S. Senate, 1974–1984: Party Change and Institutional Development*. New York: Manchester University Press, 1988.

Baker, Richard A. *The Senate of the United States: A Bicentennial History*. Malabar, FL: R.E. Krieger, 1988.

Baker, Ross K. *Friend and Foe in the U.S. Senate*. New York: Free Press, 1980.

Bolling, Richard. *House Out of Order*. New York: Dutton, 1965.

———. *Power in the House: A History of the Leadership of the House of Representatives*. New York: Capricorn Books, 1974.

Burdette, Franklin L. *Filibustering in the Senate*. Princeton, NJ: Princeton University Press, 1940.

Burns, James M. *Congress on Trial: Legislative Process and the Administrative State*. New York: Harper and Row, 1949.

Clark, Joseph S., et al. *The Senate Establishment*. New York: Hill and Wang, 1963.

Cooper, Joseph, and G. Calvin Mackenzie, eds. *The House at Work*. Austin: University of Texas Press, 1981.

Currie, James T. *The United States House of Representatives*. Malabar, FL: R.E. Krieger, 1988.

Foley, Michael. *The New Senate: Liberal Influence on a Conservative Institution, 1959–1972*. New Haven, CT: Yale University Press, 1980.

Freidin, Seymour. *A Sense of the Senate*. New York: Dodd, Mead, 1972.

Galloway, George B., and Sidney Wise, eds. *History of the House of Representatives*. 2d ed. New York: Crowell, 1976.

Harris, Fred R. *Deadlock or Decision: The U.S. Senate and the Rise of National Politics*. New York: Oxford University Press, 1993.

Haynes, George H. *The Senate of the United States*. Boston: Houghton Mifflin, 1938.

Hibbing, John R., ed. *The Changing World of the U.S. Senate*. Berkeley, CA: IGS Press, 1990.

Hinckley, Barbara. *The Seniority System in Congress*. Bloomington: Indiana University Press, 1971.

Hurst, Louis, and Frances S. Leighton. *The Sweetest Little Club in the World: The U.S. Senate*. Englewood Cliffs, NJ: Prentice-Hall, 1980.

Lodge, Henry C. *The Senate of the United States and Other Essays*. New York: Scribner's, 1921.

MacNeil, Neil. *Forge of Democracy: The House of Representatives*. New York: McKay, 1963.

Oleszek, Walter J. *Congressional Procedures and the Policy Process*. 4th ed. Washington, DC: CQ Press, 1995.

Peabody, Robert L., and Nelson W. Polsby, eds. *New Perspectives on the House of Representatives*. 4th ed. Baltimore: Johns Hopkins University Press, 1992.

Preston, Nathaniel S., ed. *The Senate Institution*. New York: Van Nostrand, 1969.

Reedy, George. *The U.S. Senate: Paralysis or a Search for Consensus?* New York: Crown, 1986.

Ripley, Randall B. *Power in the Senate*. New York: St. Martin's Press, 1969.

Rogers, Lindsay. *The American Senate*. New York: Knopf, 1926.

Rosenthal, Alan. *Toward Majority Rule in the United States Senate*. New York: McGraw-Hill, 1962.

Rothman, David J. *Politics and Power: The United States Senate, 1869–1901*. Cambridge, MA: Harvard University Press, 1966.

Sinclair, Barbara. *Legislators, Leaders, and Lawmaking: The U.S. House of Representatives in the Postreform Era*. Baltimore: Johns Hopkins University Press, 1995.

———. *The Transformation of the U.S. Senate*. Baltimore: Johns Hopkins University Press, 1989.

Sullivan, Terry O. *Procedural Structure: Success and Influence in Congress*. New York: Praeger, 1984.

White, William S. *Citadel: The Story of the U.S. Senate*. New York: Harper and Row, 1957.

———. *Home Plate: The Story of the U.S. House of Representatives*. Boston: Houghton Mifflin, 1965.

Congressional Reform

Benjamin, Gerald, and Michael J. Malbin, eds. *Limiting Legislative Terms*. Washington, DC: CQ Press, 1992.

Clark, Joseph S., ed. *Congressional Reform: Problems and Prospects*. New York: Crowell, 1965.

Crane, Edward H., and Roger Pilon, eds. *The Politics and Law of Term Limits*. Washington, DC: Cato Institute, 1994.

Davidson, Roger H., ed. *The Postreform Congress*. New York: St. Martin's Press, 1992.

Davidson, Roger H., David M. Kovenock, and Michael K. O'Leary. *Congress in Crisis: Politics and Congressional Reform*. Belmont, CA: Wadsworth, 1966.

Galloway, George B. *Next Steps in Congressional Reform*. Urbana: University of Illinois Press, 1952.

Heller, Robert. *Strengthening the Congress*. Washington, DC: National Planning Association, 1945.

———. *Strengthening the Congress: A Progress Report*. Washington, DC: National Planning Association, 1947.

Lambro, Donald. *Washington—City of Scandals: Investigating Congress and Other Big Spenders*. Boston: Little, Brown, 1984.

Rhodes, John J. *The Futile System: How to Unchain Congress and Make the System Work Again*. Garden City, NJ: Doubleday, 1976.

Rieselbach, Leroy N. *Congressional Reform in the Seventies*. Morristown, NJ: General Learning Press, 1977.

———. *Congressional Reform: The Changing Modern Congress*. Washington, DC: CQ Press, 1994.

———, ed. *Legislative Reform: The Policy Impact*. Lexington, MA: Lexington Books, 1978.

Thurber, James A., and Roger H. Davidson, eds. *Remaking Congress: Change and Stability in the 1990s*. Washington, DC: Congressional Quarterly, 1995.

Welch, Susan, and John Peters, eds. *Legislative Reform and Public Policy*. New York: Praeger, 1977.

Will, George F. *Restoration: Congress, Term Limits, and the Recovery of Deliberative Democracy*. New York: Free Press, 1992.

Powers of Congress

Aberbach, Joel D. *Keeping a Watchful Eye: The Politics of Congressional Oversight.* Washington, DC: Brookings Institution, 1990.

Berger, Raoul. *Impeachment: The Constitutional Problems.* Cambridge, MA: Harvard University Press, 1973.

Berkman, Michael B. *The State Roots of National Politics: Congress and the Tax Agenda, 1978–1986.* Pittsburgh: University of Pittsburgh Press, 1993.

Black, Charles L. *Impeachment: A Handbook.* New Haven, CT: Yale University Press, 1974.

Brant, Irving. *Impeachment: Trials and Errors.* New York: Knopf, 1972.

Foreman, Christopher H., Jr. *Signals from the Hill: Congressional Oversight and the Challenge of Social Regulation.* New Haven, CT: Yale University Press, 1988.

Franklin, Daniel P. *Making Ends Meet: Congressional Budgeting in the Age of Deficits.* Washington, DC: Congressional Quarterly, 1993.

Gilmour, John B. *Reconciliable Differences? Congress, the Budget Process, and the Deficit.* Berkeley: University of California, 1990.

Harris, Charles W. *Congress and the Governance of the Nation's Capital.* Washington, DC: Georgetown University Press, 1995.

Harris, Joseph P. *The Advise and Consent of the Senate: A Study of the Confirmation of Appointments by the United States Senate.* Berkeley: University of California Press, 1953.

Havemann, Joel. *Congress and the Budget.* Bloomington: Indiana University Press, 1978.

Huzar, Elias. *The Purse and the Sword: Control of the Army by Congress Through Military Appropriations, 1933–1950.* Ithaca, NY: Cornell University Press, 1950.

Ippolito, Dennis S. *Congressional Spending.* Ithaca, NY: Cornell University Press, 1981.

Kurland, Philip B. *Watergate and the Constitution.* Chicago: Chicago University Press, 1978.

Labovitz, John R. *Presidential Impeachment.* New Haven, CT: Yale University Press, 1978.

LeLoup, Lance T. *Budgetary Politics: Dollars, Deficits, Decisions.* Brunswick, OH: King's Court Communications, 1977.

———. *The Fiscal Congress: Legislative Control of the Budget.* Westport, CT: Greenwood Press, 1980.

Marini, John A. *The Politics of Budget Control: Congress, the Presidency, and the Growth of the Administrative State.* New York: Crane Russak, 1992.

Massaro, John. *Supremely Political: The Role of Ideology and Presidential Management in Unsuccessful Supreme Court Nominations.* New York: State University of New York Press, 1990.

Ogul, Morris S. *Congress Oversees the Bureaucracy: Studies in Legislative Supervision.* Pittsburgh: University of Pittsburgh Press, 1976.

Penner, Rudolph G., and Alan J. Abramson. *Broken Purse Strings: Congressional Budgeting 1974–1988.* Washington, DC: Urban Institute Press, 1988.

Pfiffner, James P. *The President, the Budget and Congress: Impoundment and the 1974 Budget Act.* Boulder, CO: Westview Press, 1979.

Pressman, Jeffry L. *House vs. Senate: Conflict in the Appropriations Process.* New Haven, CT: Yale University Press, 1966.

Saloma, John S. *The Responsible Use of Power: A Critical Analysis of the Congressional Budget Process.* Washington, DC: American Enterprise Institute for Public Policy Research, 1964.

Schick, Allen. *Congress and Money: Budgeting, Spending, and Taxing.* Washington, DC: Urban Institute Press, 1980.

Schmeckebier, Laurence F. *The District of Columbia: Its Government and Administration.* Baltimore: Johns Hopkins University Press, 1928.

Schoenbrod, David. *Power without Responsibility: How Congress Abuses the People through Delegation.* New Haven, CT: Yale University Press, 1993.

Shuman, Howard E. *Politics and the Budget: The Struggle between the President and the Congress.* 3d ed. Englewood Cliffs, NJ: Prentice Hall, 1992.

Simon, Paul. *Advice and Consent: Clarence Thomas, Robert Bork, and the Intriguing History of the Supreme Court's Nomination Battles.* Washington, DC: National Press Book, 1992.

Thompson, Charles S. *An Essay on the Rise and Fall of the Congressional Caucus as a Machine for Nominating Candidates for the Presidency.* New Haven, CT: Yale University Press, 1902.

Wallace, Robert A. *Congressional Control of Federal Spending.* Detroit: Wayne State University Press, 1960.

Wander, W. Thomas, F. Ted Herbert, and Gary W. Copeland, eds. *Congressional Budgeting: Politics, Process, and Power.* Baltimore: Johns Hopkins University Press, 1984.

White, Joseph, and Aaron Wildavsky. *The Deficit and the Public Interest: The Search for Responsible Budgeting in the 1980s.* Berkeley: University of California Press, 1989.

Wildavsky, Aaron B. *The New Politics of the Budgetary Process.* 2d ed. New York: HarperCollins, 1992.

———. *The Politics of the Budgetary Process.* 4th ed. Boston: Little, Brown, 1984.

Wilmerding, Lucius. *The Spending Power: A History of the Efforts of Congress to Control Expenditures.* New Haven, CT: Yale University Press, 1943.

Congressional Investigations

Barth, Alan. *Government by Investigation.* New York: Viking, 1955.

Berger, Raoul. *Executive Privilege: A Constitutional Myth.* Cambridge, MA: Harvard University Press, 1974.

Carr, Robert K. *The House Committee on Un-American Activities, 1945–1950.* Ithaca, NY: Cornell University Press, 1952.

Dimock, Marshall E. *Congressional Investigating Committees.* Baltimore: Johns Hopkins University Press, 1929.

Eberling, Ernest J. *Congressional Investigations: A Study of the Origin and Development of the Power of Congress to Investigate and Punish for Contempt.* New York: Columbia University Press, 1928.

Goldfarb, Ronald L. *The Contempt Power.* New York: Columbia University Press, 1963.

Goodman, Walter. *The Committee: The Extraordinary Career of the House Committee on Un-American Activities.* New York: Farrar, Strauss, and Giroux, 1968.

Hamilton, James. *The Power to Probe: A Study of Congressional Investigations.* New York: Random House, 1976.

Moore, William H. *The Kefauver Committee and the Politics of Crime, 1950–1952.* Columbia: University of Missouri Press, 1974.

Riddle, Donald H. *The Truman Committee: A Study in Congressional Responsibility.* New Brunswick, NJ: Rutgers University Press, 1964.

Schlesinger, Arthur M., and Roger Burns. *Congress Investigates: A Documented History 1792–1974.* New York: Chelsea House, 1975.

Taylor, Telford. *Grand Inquest: The Story of Congressional Investigations.* New York: Simon and Schuster, 1955.

Foreign Relations

Abshire, David M. *Foreign Policy Makers: President vs. Congress.* Beverly Hills, CA: Sage Publications, 1979.

Abshire, David M., and Ralph D. Nurnberger. *The Growing Power of Congress.* Beverly Hills, CA: Sage Publications, 1981.

Bauer, Raymond A., Ithiel de Sola Pool, and Lewis A. Dexter. *American Business and Public Policy: The Politics of Foreign Trade.* 2d ed. New York: Atherton Press, 1982.

Blechman, Barry M. *The Politics of National Security: Congress and U.S. Defense Policy.* New York: Oxford University Press, 1990.

Carroll, Holbert N. *The House of Representatives and Foreign Affairs.* Rev. ed. Boston: Little, Brown, 1966.

Colegrove, Kenneth S. *The American Senate and World Peace.* New York: Vanguard Press, 1944.

Crabb, Cecil V., Jr. *Invitation to Struggle: Congress, the President, and Foreign Policy.* 4th ed. Washington, DC: CQ Press, 1992.

Dahl, Robert A. *Congress and Foreign Policy.* New York: Harcourt, Brace and World, 1950.

Dangerfield, Royden J., and Quincy Wright. *In Defense of the Senate: A Study in Treaty Making.* Norman: University of Oklahoma Press, 1933.

Feuerwerger, Marvin C. *Congress and Israel: Foreign Aid Decision-Making in the House of Representatives, 1969–1976.* Westport, CT: Greenwood Press, 1979.

Fleming, Denna F. *The Treaty Veto of the American Senate.* New York: G.P. Putnam's Sons, 1930.

Franck, Thomas M., ed. *The Tethered Presidency: Congressional Restraints on Executive Power.* New York: New York University Press, 1981.

Frye, Alton. *A Responsible Congress: The Politics of National Security.* New York: McGraw-Hill, 1975.

Gallagher, Hugh G. *Advise and Obstruct: The Role of the United States Senate in Foreign Policy Decisions.* New York: Delacorte Press, 1969.

Hayden, Joseph R. *The Senate and Treaties, 1789–1817: The Development of the Treaty Making Functions of the United States Senate During Their Formative Period.* New York: Macmillan, 1920.

Hinckley, Barbara. *Less Than Meets the Eye: Foreign Policymaking and the Myth of the Assertive Congress.* Chicago: University of Chicago Press, 1994.

Holt, Pat M. *The War Powers Resolution: The Role of Congress in Armed Intervention.* Washington, DC: American Enterprise Institute for Public Policy Research, 1978.

Holt, William S. *Treaties Defeated by the Senate: A Study of the Struggle between President and Senate over the Conduct of Foreign Relations.* Baltimore: Johns Hopkins University Press, 1933.

Hughes, Kent H. *International Economic Decision Making in Congress: Trade, Taxes, and Transnationals.* New York: Praeger, 1979.

Javits, Jacob K., and Don Kellerman. *Who Makes War: The President Versus Congress.* New York: William Morrow and Company, 1973.

Jewell, Malcolm E. *Senatorial Politics and Foreign Policy.* Lexington: University Press of Kentucky, 1962.

Johnson, Loch K. *The Making of International Agreements: Congress Confronts the Executive.* New York: New York University Press, 1984.

Kellor, Frances A., and Antonia Hatvany. *The United States Senate and the International Court.* New York: T. Seltzer, 1925.

Keynes, Edward. *Undeclared War: Twilight Zone of Constitutional Power.* University Park: Pennsylvania State University Press, 1982.

Lehman, John F. *The Executive, Congress, and Foreign Policy: Studies of the Nixon Administration.* New York: Praeger, 1976.

Lindsay, James M. *Congress and Nuclear Weapons.* Baltimore: Johns Hopkins University Press, 1991.

———. *Congress and the Politics of U.S. Foreign Policy.* Baltimore: Johns Hopkins University Press, 1994.

Liske, Craig, and Barry S. Rundquist. *The Politics of Weapons Procurement: The Role of Congress.* Denver: University of Colorado, 1974.

Lodge, Henry C. *The Senate and the League of Nations.* New York: Scribner's, 1925.

Pastor, Robert A. *Congress and the Politics of U.S. Foreign Economic Policy, 1926–1976.* Berkeley: University of California Press, 1980.

Platt, Alan. *The U.S. Senate and Strategic Arms Policy, 1969–1977.* Boulder, CO: Westview Press, 1978.

Platt, Alan, and Lawrence D. Weiler, eds. *Congress and Arms Control.* Boulder, CO: Westview Press, 1978.

Reveley, W. Taylor, III. *War Powers of the President and Congress: Who Holds the Arrows and Olive Branch?* Charlottesville: University Press of Virginia, 1981.

Ripley, Randall B., and James M. Lindsay, eds. *Congress Resurgent: Foreign and Defense Policy on Capitol Hill.* Ann Arbor: University of Michigan Press, 1993.

Rourke, John T. *Congress and the Presidency in U.S. Foreign Policymaking: A Study of Interaction and Influence, 1945–1982.* Boulder, CO: Westview Press, 1983.

Sofaer, Abraham D. *War, Foreign Affairs and Constitution Power: The Origins.* Cambridge, MA: Ballinger, 1976.

Spanier, John W., and Joseph L. Nogee, eds. *Congress, the Presidency, and American Foreign Policy.* New York: Pergamon Press, 1981.

Stennis, John C., and J. William Fulbright. *The Role of Congress in Foreign Policy.* Washington, DC: American Enterprise Institute for Public Policy Research, 1971.

Warburg, Gerald F. *Conflict and Consensus: The Struggle between Congress and the President over Foreign Policymaking.* New York: Ballinger, 1989.

Weissman, Stephen R. *A Culture of Deference: Congress and the Making of American Foreign Policy.* New York: Basic Books, 1995.

Whalen, Charles W., Jr. *The House and Foreign Policy: The Irony of Congressional Reform.* Chapel Hill: University of North Carolina Press, 1982.

Wilcox, John C. *Congress, The Executive and Foreign Policy.* New York: Harper and Row, 1971.

Committee Structure and Work

Collier, Ellen C. *Postwar Presidents and the Senate Foreign Relations Committee.* Washington, DC: Legislative Reference Service, 1969.

Cooper, Joseph. *Origins of the Standing Committees and Development of the Modern House*. Houston: Rice University, 1971.

Dennison, Eleanor E. *The Senate Foreign Relations Committee*. Stanford, CA: Stanford University Press, 1942.

Evans, C. Lawrence. *Leadership in Committee: A Comparative Analysis of Leadership Behavior in the U.S. Senate*. Ann Arbor: University of Michigan Press, 1991.

Farnsworth, David N. *The Senate Committee on Foreign Relations: A Study of the Decision-Making Process*. Urbana: University of Illinois Press, 1961.

Fenno, Richard F. *Congressmen in Committees*. Boston: Little, Brown, 1973.

———. *The Power of the Purse: Appropriation Politics in Congress*. Boston: Little, Brown, 1966.

Ferejohn, John A. *Pork Barrel Politics: Rivers and Harbors Legislation, 1947–1968*. Stanford, CA: Stanford University Press, 1974.

Goodwin, George. *The Little Legislatures: Committees of Congress*. Amherst: University of Massachusetts Press, 1970.

Green, Harold P. *Government of the Atom: The Integration of Powers*. New York: Atherton Press, 1963.

Henderson, Thomas A. *Congressional Oversight of Executive Agencies: A Study of the House Committee on Government Operations*. Gainesville: University of Florida Press, 1970.

Horn, Stephen. *Unused Power: The Work of the Senate Committee on Appropriations*. Washington, DC: Brookings Institution, 1970.

Kammerer, Gladys M. *The Staffing of the Committees of Congress*. Lexington: University Press of Kentucky, 1949.

Lees, John D. *The Committee System of the United States Congress*. New York: Humanities Press, 1967.

Longley, Lawrence D., and Walter J. Oleszek. *Bicameral Politics: Conference Committees in Congress*. New Haven, CT: Yale University Press, 1989.

Manley, John F. *The Politics of Finance: The House Committee on Ways and Means.* Boston: Little, Brown, 1970.

Matsunaga, Spark M., and Ping Chen. *Rulemakers of the House.* Urbana: University of Illinois Press, 1976.

McConachie, Lauros G. *Congressional Committees.* New York: Crowell, 1898.

McGown, Ada C. *The Congressional Conference Committee.* New York: Columbia University Press, 1927.

Morrow, William L. *Congressional Committees.* New York: Scribner's, 1969.

Munson, Richard. *The Cardinals of Capitol Hill: The Men and Women Who Control Federal Spending.* New York: Grove Press, 1993.

Murphy, Thomas P. *The Politics of Congressional Committees: The Power of Seniority.* Woodbury, NY: Barron's, 1978.

Parker, Glenn R., and Suzanne L. Parker. *Factions in House Committees.* Knoxville: University of Tennessee Press, 1985.

Price, David E. *Who Makes the Laws? Creativity and Power in Senate Committees.* Cambridge, MA: Schenkman, 1972.

Reeves, Andree E. *Congressional Committee Chairmen: Three Who Made an Evolution.* Lexington: University of Kentucky Press, 1993.

Robinson, James A. *The House Rules Committee.* Indianapolis: Bobbs-Merrill, 1963.

Shepsle, Kenneth A. *The Giant Jigsaw Puzzle: Democratic Committee Assignments in the Modern House.* Chicago: Chicago University Press, 1978.

Siff, Ted, and Alan Weil, eds. *Ruling Congress: A Study on How the House and Senate Rules Govern the Legislative Process.* New York: Grossman, 1975.

Smith, Steven S., and Christopher J. Deering. *Committees in Congress.* 2d ed. Washington, DC: CQ Press, 1990.

Steiner, Gilbert Y. *The Congressional Conference Committee: Seventieth to Eightieth Congresses.* Urbana: University of Illinois Press, 1951.

Strahan, Randall Wayne. *New Ways and Means: Reform and Change in a Congressional Committee.* Chapel Hill: University of North Carolina Press, 1990.

Unekis, Joseph K., and Leroy N. Rieselbach. *Congressional Committee Politics: Continuity and Change.* New York: Praeger, 1984.

Uslaner, Eric M. *Congressional Committee Assignments: Alternative Models for Behavior.* Beverly Hills, CA: Sage Publications, 1974.

Vogler, David J. *The Third House: Conference Committees in the United States Congress.* Evanston, IL: Northwestern University Press, 1971.

Westphal, Albert C. *The House Committee on Foreign Affairs.* New York: Columbia University Press, 1942.

Legislative Analysis

Alexander, Thomas B. *Sectional Stress and Party Strength: A Study of Roll-Call Voting in the United States House of Representatives, 1830–1860.* Nashville, TN: Vanderbilt University, 1967.

Anderson, Lee F., Meredith W. Watts, and Allen R. Wilcox. *Legislative Roll-Call Analysis.* Evanston, IL: Northwestern University Press, 1966.

Arnold, R. Douglas. *The Logic of Congressional Action.* New Haven, CT: Yale University Press, 1990.

Bell, Rudolph M. *Party and Faction in American Politics: The House of Representatives, 1789–1801.* Westport, CT: Greenwood Press, 1973.

Bernstein, Robert A. *Elections, Representation, and Congressional Voting Behavior: The Myth of Constituency Control.* Englewood Cliffs, NJ: Prentice-Hall, 1989.

Brady, David W. *Congressional Voting in a Partisan Era: A Study of the McKinley Houses and a Comparison to the Modern House of Representatives.* Lawrence: University of Kansas Press, 1973.

Clausen, Aage R. *How Congressmen Decide: A Policy Focus.* New York: St. Martin's Press, 1973.

Cox, Gary W., and Samuel Kernell, eds. *The Politics of Divided Government.* Boulder, CO: Westview Press, 1992.

Fiorina, Morris P. *Divided Government.* New York: Macmillan, 1992.

Froman, Lewis A. *The Congressional Process: Strategies, Rules and Procedures.* Boston: Little, Brown, 1967.

Galloway, George B. *The Legislative Process in Congress.* New York: Crowell, 1953.

Jackson, John E. *Constituencies and Leaders in Congress: Their Effects on Senate Voting Behavior.* Cambridge, MA: Harvard University Press, 1974.

Johannes, John R. *Policy Innovation in Congress.* Morristown, NJ: General Learning Press, 1972.

Kau, James B., and Paul H. Rubin. *Congressmen, Constituents, and Contributors: Determinants of Roll Call Voting in the House of Representatives.* Hingham, MA: Martinus Nijhoff, 1982.

Kingdon, John W. *Congressmen's Voting Decisions.* 3d ed. Ann Arbor: University of Michigan Press, 1989.

Luce, Robert. *Legislative Principles: The History and Theory of Law-Making by Representative Government.* Boston: Houghton Mifflin, 1930.

MacRae, Duncan. *Dimensions of Congressional Voting: A Statistical Study of the House of Representatives in the Eighty-First Congress.* Berkeley: University of California Press, 1958.

Parker, Glenn R. *Characteristics of Congress: Patterns in Congressional Behavior.* Englewood Cliffs, NJ: Prentice Hall, 1989.

———. *Institutional Change, Discretion, and the Making of Modern Congress: An Economic Interpretation.* Ann Arbor: University of Michigan Press, 1992.

Polsby, Nelson W., ed. *Congressional Behavior.* New York: Random House, 1971.

Schneider, Jerrold E. *Ideological Coalitions in Congress.* Westport, CT: Greenwood Press, 1979.

Shannon, W. Wayne. *Party, Constituency and Congressional Voting*. Baton Rouge: Louisiana State University Press, 1968.

Silbey, Joel H. *The Shrine of Party: Congressional Voting Behavior, 1841–1852*. Pittsburgh: University of Pittsburgh Press, 1967.

Sinclair, Barbara. *Congressional Realignment, 1925–1978*. Austin: University of Texas Press, 1982.

Smith, Steven S. *Call to Order: Floor Politics in the House and Senate*. Washington, DC: Brookings Institution, 1989.

Strom, Gerald S. *The Logic of Lawmaking: A Spatial Theory Approach*. Baltimore: Johns Hopkins University Press, 1990.

Turner, Julius, and Edward V. Schneier. *Party and Constituency: Pressures on Congress*. Rev. ed. Baltimore: Johns Hopkins University Press, 1970.

Vogler, David J., and Sidney R. Waldman. *Congress and Democracy*. Washington, DC: CQ Press, 1985.

Wahlke, John C., and Heinz Eulau. *Legislative Behavior: A Reader in Theory and Research*. New York: Free Press, 1959.

Zinn, Charles J. *American Congressional Procedure*. St. Paul, MN: West Publishing Co., 1957.

Legislative Case Studies

Bailey, Stephen K. *Congress Makes a Law: The Story Behind the Employment Act of 1946*. New York: Columbia University Press, 1950.

Bardach, Eugene. *The Implementation Game: What Happens After a Bill Becomes Law*. Cambridge, MA: MIT Press, 1977.

Bendiner, Robert. *Obstacle Course on Capitol Hill*. New York: McGraw-Hill, 1964.

Berman, Daniel M. *A Bill Becomes Law: The Civil Rights Act of 1960*. New York: Macmillan, 1962.

Brezina, Dennis W. *Congress in Action: The Environmental Education Act*. New York: Free Press, 1974.

Cleaveland, Frederic N., et al. *Congress and Urban Problems: A Casebook on the Legislative Process*. Washington, DC: Brookings Institution, 1969.

Cooley, Richard A., and Geoffrey Wandesforde-Smith, eds. *Congress and the Environment*. Seattle: University of Washington Press, 1970.

Eidenberg, Eugene, and Roy D. Morey. *An Act of Congress: The Legislative Process and the Making of Education Policy*. New York: W.W. Norton, 1969.

Gross, Bertram M. *The Legislative Struggle: A Study in Social Combat*. New York: McGraw-Hill, 1953.

Levine, Erwin L., and Elizabeth M. Wexler. *PL 94-142: An Act of Congress*. New York: Macmillan, 1981.

Munger, Frank J., and Richard F. Fenno. *National Politics and Federal Aid to Education*. Syracuse, NY: Syracuse University Press, 1962.

Olson, David M. *The Politics of Legislation: A Congressional Simulation*. New York: Praeger, 1976.

Redman, Eric. *The Dance of Legislation*. New York: Simon and Schuster, 1973.

Schick, Allen, ed. *Making Economic Policy in Congress*. Washington, DC: American Enterprise Institute for Public Policy Research, 1983.

Schier, Steven E. *A Decade of Deficits: Congressional Thought and Fiscal Action*. Albany: State University of New York Press, 1992.

Shull, Steven A. *Domestic Policy Formation: Presidential-Congressional Partnership?* Westport, CT: Greenwood Press, 1983.

Thomas, Morgan. *Atomic Energy and Congress*. Ann Arbor: University of Michigan Press, 1956.

VanDoren, Peter M. *Politics, Markets, and Congressional Policy Choices*. Ann Arbor: University of Michigan Press, 1991.

West, Darrell M. *Congress and Economic Policymaking*. Pittsburgh: University of Pittsburgh Press, 1987.

Leadership in Congress

Bibby, John F. *Politics, Parties, and Elections in America.* 2d ed. Chicago: Nelson-Hall, 1992.

Bolling, Richard. *Defeating the Leadership Nominee in the House Democratic Caucus.* Indianapolis: Bobbs-Merrill, 1965.

Cheney, Richard B., and Lynne V. Cheney. *Kings of the Hill: Power and Personality in the House of Representatives.* New York: Continuum, 1983.

Chiu, Chang-Wei. *The Speaker of the House of Representatives Since 1896.* New York: Columbia University Press, 1928.

Connelly, William F., Jr., and John J. Pitney, Jr. *Congress' Permanent Minority? Republicans in the U.S. House.* Lanham, MD: Rowman and Littlefield, 1994.

Cox, Gary W., and Mathew D. McCubbins. *Legislative Leviathan: Party Government in the House.* Berkeley: University of California Press, 1993.

Follett, Mary P. *The Speaker of the House of Representatives.* New York: Longmans, Green, 1896.

Fuller, Hubert B. *The Speakers of the House.* Boston: Little, Brown, 1909.

Hasbrouck, Paul D. *Party Government in the House of Representatives.* New York: Macmillan, 1927.

Holt, James. *Congressional Insurgents and the Party System, 1909–1916.* Cambridge, MA: Harvard University Press, 1967.

Jones, Charles O. *The Minority Party in Congress.* Boston: Little, Brown, 1970.

———. *Party and Policy-Making: The House Republican Policy Committee.* New Brunswick, NJ: Rutgers University Press, 1964.

Kiewiet, D. Roderick, and Mathew D. McCubbins. *The Logic of Delegation: Congressional Parties and the Appropriations Process.* Chicago: University of Chicago Press, 1991.

Kornacki, John J., ed. *Leading Congress: New Styles, New Strategies*. Washington, DC: Congressional Quarterly, 1990.

Mackaman, Frank H., ed. *Understanding Congressional Leadership*. Washington, DC: CQ Press, 1981.

Maxwell, Neal A. *Regionalism in the United States Senate: The West*. Salt Lake City: Institute of Government, University of Utah, 1961.

Mayhew, David R. *Divided We Govern: Party Control, Lawmaking, and Investigations 1946–1990*. New Haven, CT: Yale University Press, 1991.

———. *Party Loyalty Among Congressmen: The Difference between Democrats and Republicans, 1947–1962*. Cambridge, MA: Harvard University Press, 1966.

McCune, Wesley. *The Farm Bloc*. Garden City, NJ: Doubleday, 1943.

Palazzolo, Daniel J. *The Speaker and the Budget: Leadership in the Post-Reform House of Representatives*. Pittsburgh: University of Pittsburgh Press, 1992.

Peabody, Robert L. *Leadership in Congress: Stability, Succession, and Change*. Boston: Little, Brown, 1976.

Peters, Ronald M., Jr. *The American Speakership: The Office in Historical Perspective*. Baltimore: Johns Hopkins University Press, 1990.

———, ed. *The Speaker: Leadership in the U.S. House of Representatives*. Washington, DC: Congressional Quarterly, 1994.

Ripley, Randall B. *Majority Party Leadership in Congress*. Boston: Little, Brown, 1969.

———. *Party Leaders in the House of Representatives*. Washington, DC: Brookings Institution, 1967.

Rohde, David W. *Parties and Leaders in the Postreform House*. Chicago: University of Chicago Press, 1991.

Schattschneider, Elmer E. *Party Government*. New York: Holt, Rinehart, and Winston, 1942.

Shaffer, William R. *Party and Ideology in the United States Congress.* Lanham, MD: University Press of America, 1980.

Sinclair, Barbara. *Majority Leadership in the U.S. House.* Baltimore: Johns Hopkins University Press, 1983.

Truman, David B. *The Congressional Party: A Case Study.* New York: Wiley, 1959.

Pressures on Congress

Arnold, R. Douglas. *Congress and the Bureaucracy: A Theory of Influence.* New Haven, CT: Yale University Press, 1979.

Berger, Raoul. *Congress vs. the Supreme Court.* Cambridge, MA: Harvard University Press, 1969.

Binkley, Wilfred E. *President and Congress.* 3d ed. New York: Vintage, 1962.

Black, Henry C. *The Relation of the Executive Power to Legislation.* Princeton, NJ: Princeton University Press, 1919.

Blanchard, Robert O., ed. *Congress and the News Media.* New York: Hastings House, 1974.

Bond, Jon R., and Richard Fleisher. *The President in the Legislative Arena.* Chicago: University of Chicago Press, 1990.

Bowles, Nigel. *The White House and Capitol Hill: The Politics of Presidential Persuasion.* New York: Oxford University Press, 1987.

Breckenridge, Adam C. *Congress against the Court.* Lincoln: University of Nebraska Press, 1970.

Burns, James M. *The Deadlock of Democracy: Four-Party Politics in America.* Rev. ed. Englewood Cliffs, NJ: Prentice-Hall, 1967.

Cain, Bruce E., John A. Ferejohn, and Morris P. Fiorina. *The Personal Vote: Constituency Service and Electoral Independence.* Cambridge, MA: Harvard University Press, 1987.

Chamberlain, Lawrence H. *The President, Congress, and Legislation.* New York: Columbia University Press, 1946.

Clarke, Peter, and Susan H. Evans. *Covering Campaigns: Journalism in Congressional Elections*. Stanford, CA: Stanford University Press, 1983.

Clawson, Dan, Alan Neustadtl, and Denise Scott. *Money Talks: Corporate PACs and Political Influence*. New York: Basic Books, 1992.

Congressional Quarterly. *The Washington Lobby*. 5th ed. Washington, DC: Congressional Quarterly, 1987.

Cook, Timothy E. *Making Laws and Making News: Media Strategies in the U.S. House of Representatives*. Washington, DC: Brookings Institution, 1989.

Davis, James W., and Delbert Rinquist. *The President and Congress: Toward a New Balance*. Woodbury, NY: Barron's, 1975.

De Grazia, Alfred. *Republic in Crisis: Congress Against the Executive Force*. New York: Federal Legal Publication, 1965.

Edwards, George C., III. *At the Margins: Presidential Leadership of Congress*. New Haven, CT: Yale University Press, 1989.

———. *Presidential Influence in Congress*. San Francisco: W.H. Freeman, 1980.

Eggers, Rowland A., and Joseph P. Harris. *The President and Congress*. New York: McGraw-Hill, 1963.

Fenno, Richard F. *Home Style: House Members in Their Districts*. Boston: Little, Brown, 1978.

Fiorina, Morris P. *Representatives, Roll Calls and Constituencies*. Lexington, MA: Lexington Books, 1974.

Fiorina, Morris P., and David W. Rohde, eds. *Home Style and Washington Work: Studies of Congressional Politics*. Ann Arbor: University of Michigan Press, 1989.

Fisher, Louis. *The Politics of Shared Power: Congress and the Executive*. 3d ed. Washington, DC: CQ Press, 1993.

———. *President and Congress: Power and Policy*. New York: Free Press, 1972.

Freeman, J. Leiper. *The Political Process: Executive Bureau-Legislative Committee Relations*. Rev. ed. New York: Random House, 1965.

Froman, Lewis A. *The Congressmen and Their Constituencies*. Chicago: Rand McNally, 1963.

Hansen, John M. *Gaining Access: Congress and the Farm Lobby*. Chicago: University of Chicago Press, 1991.

Harris, Joseph P. *Congressional Control of Administration*. Washington, DC: Brookings Institution, 1964.

Herring, Edward P. *Presidential Leadership: The Political Relations of Congress and the Chief Executive*. New York: Farrar and Rinehart, 1940.

Hess, Stephen. *Live from Capitol Hill!: Studies of Congress and the Media*. Washington, DC: Brookings Institution, 1991.

———. *The Ultimate Insiders: U.S. Senators in the National Media*. Washington, DC: Brookings Institution, 1986.

Hibbing, John R. *Congress as Public Enemy: Public Attitudes toward American Political Institutions*. New York: Cambridge University Press, 1995.

Holtzman, Abraham. *Legislative Liaison: Executive Leadership in Congress*. Chicago: Rand McNally, 1970.

Horn, Stephen. *The Cabinet and Congress*. New York: Columbia University Press, 1960.

Johannes, John R. *To Serve the People: Congress and Constituency Service*. Lincoln: University of Nebraska Press, 1984.

Johnson, Cathy M. *The Dynamics of Conflict between Bureaucrats and Legislators*. Armonk, NY: M.E. Sharpe, 1992.

Jones, Charles O. *Separate But Equal Branches: Congress and the Presidency*. Chatham, NJ: Chatham House, 1995.

———. *The Trusteeship Presidency: Jimmy Carter and the United States Congress*. Baton Rouge: Louisiana State University Press, 1988.

Keynes, Edward. *The Court vs. Congress: Prayer, Busing, and Abortion*. Durham, NC: Duke University Press, 1989.

King, Anthony S., ed. *Both Ends of the Avenue: The Presidency, the Executive Branch, and Congress in the 1980s.* Washington, DC: American Enterprise Institute for Public Policy Research, 1983.

Koenig, Louis W. *Congress and the President: Official Makers of Public Policy.* Glenview, IL: Scott, Foresman, 1965.

LeLoup, Lance T., and Steven A. Shull. *Congress and the President: The Policy Connection.* Belmont, CA: Wadsworth, 1993.

Lewis, Frederick P. *The Dilemma in the Congressional Power to Enforce the Fourteenth Amendment.* Washington, DC: University Press of America, 1980.

Livingston, William S., Lawrence C. Dodd, and Richard L. Schott. *The Presidency and the Congress: A Shifting Balance of Power?* Austin: Lyndon B. Johnson School of Public Affairs, University of Texas, 1979.

Maass, Arthur. *Congress and the Common Good.* New York: Basic Books, 1983.

Mann, Thomas E., and Norman J. Ornstein. *Congress, the Press, and the Public.* Washington, DC: Brookings Institution, 1994.

Mansfield, Harvey C., ed. *Congress against the President.* New York: Academy of Political Science, 1975.

Mezey, Michael L. *Congress, the President, and Public Policy.* Boulder, CO: Westview Press, 1989.

Milbrath, Lester W. *The Washington Lobbyists.* Chicago: Rand McNally, 1963.

Moe, Ronald C., ed. *Congress and the President: Allies and Adversaries.* Pacific Palisades, CA: Goodyear, 1971.

Murphy, Thomas P. *Pressures upon Congress, Legislation by Lobby.* Woodbury, NY: Barron's, 1973.

Murphy, Walter F. *Congress and the Court: A Case Study in the American Political Process.* Chicago: University of Chicago Press, 1962.

Olson, Mancur. *The Logic of Collective Action*. Rev. ed. Cambridge, MA: Harvard University Press, 1971.

Oppenheimer, Bruce I. *Oil and the Congressional Process: The Limits of Symbolic Politics*. Lexington, MA: Lexington Books, 1974.

Ornstein, Norman J., and Shirley Elder. *Interest Groups, Lobbying and Policymaking*. Washington, DC: CQ Press, 1978.

Parker, Glenn R. *Homeward Bound: Explaining Changes in Congressional Behavior*. Pittsburgh: University of Pittsburgh Press, 1986.

————. *Political Beliefs about the Structure of Government: Congress and the Presidency*. Beverly Hills, CA: Sage Publications, 1974.

Pepper, George W. *Family Quarrels: The President, the Senate, the House*. New York: Baker, Voorhis, 1931.

Peterson, Mark A. *Legislating Together: The White House and Capitol Hill from Eisenhower to Reagan*. Cambridge, MA: Harvard University Press, 1990.

Polsby, Nelson W. *Congress and the Presidency*. 4th ed. Englewood Cliffs, NJ: Prentice-Hall, 1986.

Pritchett, C. Herman. *Congress Versus the Supreme Court 1957–1960*. Minneapolis: University of Minnesota Press, 1961.

Ritchie, Donald A. *Press Gallery: Congress and the Washington Correspondents*. Cambridge, MA: Harvard University Press, 1991.

Schlesinger, Arthur M., and Alfred De Grazia. *Congress and the Presidency: Their Role in Modern Times*. Washington, DC: American Enterprise Institute for Public Policy Research, 1967.

Schmidhauser, John R., and Larry L. Berg. *The Supreme Court and Congress: Conflict and Interaction, 1945–1968*. New York: Free Press, 1972.

Schriftgiesser, Karl. *The Lobbyists: The Art and Business of Influencing Lawmakers*. Boston: Little, Brown, 1931.

Scott, Andrew M., and Margaret A. Hunt. *Congress and Lobbies: Image and Reality*. Chapel Hill: University of North Carolina Press, 1966.

Spitzer, Robert J. *The Presidency and Public Policy: The Four Arenas of Presidential Power*. Tuscaloosa: University of Alabama Press, 1983.

————. *President and Congress: Executive Hegemony at the Crossroads of American Government*. Philadelphia: Temple University Press, 1993.

Thurber, James A., ed. *Divided Democracy: Cooperation and Conflict between the President and Congress*. Washington, DC: CQ Press, 1991.

————. *Rivals for Power: Presidential–Congressional Relations*. Washington, DC: CQ Press, 1996.

Truman, David B. *Governmental Process: Political Interests and Public Opinion*. 2d ed. New York: Knopf, 1971.

Walker, Jack L., Jr. *Mobilizing Interest Groups in America: Patrons, Professions, and Social Movements*. Ann Arbor: University of Michigan Press, 1991.

Warren, Charles. *Congress, the Constitution and the Supreme Court*. Boston: Little, Brown, 1925.

Wayne, Stephen J. *The Legislative Presidency*. New York: Harper and Row, 1978.

Wolpe, Bruce C. *Lobbying Congress: How the System Works*. Washington, DC: CQ Press, 1990.

Congress and the Electorate

Abramowitz, Alan I., and Jeffrey A. Segal. *Senate Elections*. Ann Arbor: University of Michigan Press, 1992.

Baker, Gordon E. *The Reapportionment Revolution: Representation, Political Power, and the Supreme Court*. New York: Random House, 1966.

Bone, Hugh A. *Party Committees and National Politics*. Seattle: University of Washington Press, 1968.

Brady, David W. *Critical Elections and Congressional Policy Making*. Stanford, CA: Stanford University Press, 1988.

Butler, David, and Bruce Cain. *Congressional Redistricting: Comparative and Theoretical Perspectives.* New York: Macmillan, 1992.

Campbell, James E. *The Presidential Pulse of Congressional Elections.* Lexington: University Press of Kentucky, 1993.

Clem, Alan L. *The Making of Congressmen: Seven Campaigns of 1974.* North Scituate, MA: Duxbury Press, 1976.

Coffey, Wayne R. *How We Choose a Congress.* New York: St. Martin's Press, 1980.

Common Cause. *How Money Talks in Congress: A Common Cause Study of the Impact of Money on Congressional Decision-Making.* Washington, DC: Common Cause, 1979.

Congressional Quarterly. *Congressional Campaign Finances: History, Facts, and Controversy.* Washington, DC: Congressional Quarterly, 1992.

Cooper, Joseph, and Louis S. Maisel, eds. *Congressional Elections.* Beverly Hills, CA: Sage Publications, 1981.

Cummings, Milton C. *Congressmen and the Electorate: Elections for the U.S. House and President, 1920–1964.* New York: Free Press, 1966.

Ewing, Cortez A. M. *Congressional Elections, 1896–1944: The Sectional Basis of Political Democracy in the House of Representatives.* Norman: University of Oklahoma Press, 1947.

Fishel, Jeff. *Party and Opposition: Congressional Challengers in American Politics.* New York: McKay, 1973.

———. *Representation and Responsiveness in Congress: The "Class of Eighty-Nine," 1965–1970.* Beverly Hills, CA: Sage Publications, 1973.

Fowler, Linda L. *Candidates, Congress and the American Democracy.* Ann Arbor: University of Michigan Press, 1993.

Fowler, Linda L., and Robert D. McClure. *Political Ambition: Who Decides to Run for Congress.* New Haven, CT: Yale University Press, 1989.

Fritz, Sara, and Dwight Morris. *Gold-Plated Politics: Running for Congress in the 1990s.* Washington, DC: Congressional Quarterly, 1992.

Goldenberg, Edie N., and Michael W. Traugott. *Campaigning for Congress.* Washington, DC: Congressional Quarterly, 1984.

Hacker, Andrew. *Congressional Districting: The Issue of Equal Representation.* Washington, DC: Brookings Institution, 1964.

Haynes, George H. *The Election of Senators.* New York: Holt, 1906.

Haynes, John. *Popular Elections of United States Senators.* Baltimore: Johns Hopkins University Studies, 1893.

Hinckley, Barbara. *Congressional Elections.* Washington, DC: CQ Press, 1981.

Huckshorn, Robert J., and Robert C. Spencer. *The Politics of Defeat: Campaigning for Congress.* Amherst: University of Massachusetts Press, 1971.

Jacobson, Gary C. *The Electoral Origins of Divided Government: Competition in U.S. House Elections, 1946–1988.* Boulder, CO: Westview Press, 1990.

———. *Money in Congressional Elections.* New Haven, CT: Yale University Press, 1980.

———. *The Politics of Congressional Elections.* 3d ed. New York: Harper-Collins, 1992.

Jacobson, Gary C., and Samuel Kernell. *Strategy and Choice in Congressional Elections.* New Haven, CT: Yale University Press, 1981.

Jones, Charles O. *Every Second Year: Congressional Behavior and the Two-Year Term.* Washington, DC: Brookings Institution, 1967.

Kazee, Thomas, ed. *Who Runs for Congress? Ambition, Context, and Candidate Emergence.* Washington, DC: CQ Press, 1994.

Krasno, Jonathan S. *Challengers, Competition, and Reelection: Comparing Senate and House Elections.* New Haven, CT: Yale University Press, 1994.

Kubiak, Greg D. *The Gilded Dome: The U.S. Senate and Campaign Finance Reform.* Norman: University of Oklahoma Press, 1994.

Leuthold, David A. *Electioneering in a Democracy: Campaigns for Congress.* New York: Wiley, 1968.

Magleby, David B., and Candice J. Nelson. *The Money Chase: Congressional Campaign Finance Reform.* Washington, DC: Brookings Institution, 1990.

Maisel, Louis S. *From Obscurity to Oblivion: Running in the Congressional Primary.* 2d ed. Knoxville: University of Tennessee Press, 1986.

Mann, Thomas E. *Unsafe at Any Margin: Interpreting Congressional Elections.* Washington, DC: American Enterprise Institute for Public Policy Research, 1978.

Mayhew, David R. *Congress: The Electoral Connection.* New Haven, CT: Yale University Press, 1974.

McPhee, William N., and William A. Glaser, eds. *Public Opinion and Congressional Elections.* New York: Free Press, 1962.

Miller, Warren E., and Donald E. Stokes. *Representation in Congress.* Englewood Cliffs, NJ: Prentice-Hall, 1966.

Morris, Dwight, and Murielle E. Gamache. *Gold-Plated Politics: The 1992 Congressional Races.* Washington, DC: Congressional Quarterly, 1994.

———. *Handbook of Campaign Spending: Money in the 1992 Congressional Races.* Washington, DC: Congressional Quarterly, 1994.

Nugent, Margaret L., and John R. Johannes, eds. *Money, Elections, and Democracy: Reforming Congressional Campaign Finance.* Boulder, CO: Westview Press, 1990.

Peabody, Robert L., et al. *To Enact a Law: Congress and Campaign Financing.* New York: Praeger, 1972.

Vermeer, Jan Pons, ed. *Campaigns in the News: Mass Media and Congressional Elections.* New York: Greenwood Press, 1987.

Westlye, Mark C. *Senate Elections and Campaign Intensity.* Baltimore: Johns Hopkins University Press, 1991.

Members of Congress

Asher, Herbert B. *Freshman Representatives and Learning of Voting Cues.* Beverly Hills, CA: Sage Publications, 1973.

Barber, James D. *The Lawmakers: Recruitment and Adaptation to Legislative Life*. New Haven, CT: Yale University Press, 1965.

Beard, Edmund, and Stephen Horn. *Congressional Ethics: The View from the House*. Washington, DC: Brookings Institution, 1975.

Canon, David T. *Actors, Athletes, and Astronauts: Political Amateurs in the United States Congress*. Chicago: University of Chicago Press, 1990.

Chamberlin, Hope. *A Minority of Members: Women in the U.S. Congress*. New York: Praeger, 1973.

Congressional Quarterly. *Congressional Ethics: History, Facts, and Controversy*. Washington, DC: Congressional Quarterly, 1992.

Englebarts, Rudolph. *Women in the United States Congress, 1917–1972: Their Accomplishments, with Bibliographies*. Littleton, CO: Libraries Unlimited, 1974.

Gertzog, Irwin N. *Congressional Women: Their Recruitment, Intergration, and Behavior*. 2d ed. New York: Praeger, 1995.

Getz, Robert S. *Congressional Ethics: The Conflict of Interest Issue*. Princeton, NJ: Van Nostrand, 1967.

Hibbing, John R. *Choosing to Leave: Voluntary Retirement from the U.S. House of Representatives*. Washington, DC: University Press of America, 1982.

———. *Congressional Careers: Contours of Life in the U.S. House of Representatives*. Chapel Hill: University of North Carolina Press, 1991.

Loomis, Burdett A. *The New American Politician: Ambition, Entrepreneurship, and the Changing Face of Political Life*. New York: Basic Books, 1988.

Smith, Samuel D. *The Negro in Congress, 1870–1901*. Chapel Hill: University of North Carolina Press, 1940.

Swain, Carol M. *Black Faces, Black Interests: The Representation of African Americans in Congress*. Cambridge, MA: Harvard University Press, 1993.

Thompson, Dennis F. *Ethics in Congress: From Individual to Institutional Corruption*. Washington, DC: Brookings Institutions, 1995.

Support and Housing of Congress

Chartrand, Robert L., Kenneth Janda, and Michael Hugo, eds. *Information Support, Program Budgeting and the Congress.* New York: Spartan Books, 1968.

Congressional Quarterly. *Congressional Pay and Perquisites: History, Facts, and Controversy.* Washington, DC: Congressional Quarterly, 1992.

Fox, Harrison W., and Susan W. Hammond. *Congressional Staffs: The Invisible Force in American Lawmaking.* New York: Free Press, 1977.

Frantzich, Stephen E. *Computers in Congress: The Politics of Information.* Beverly Hills, CA: Sage Publications, 1982.

Goodrum, Charles A. *The Library of Congress.* New York: Praeger, 1974.

Heaphey, James J., and Alan P. Balutis, eds. *Legislative Staffing: A Comparative Perspective.* New York: Wiley, 1975.

Kloman, Erasmus H. *Cases in Accountability: The Work of the GAO.* Boulder, CO: Westview Press, 1979.

Kofmehl, Kenneth. *Professional Staffs of Congress.* 3d ed. West Lafayette, IN: Purdue University Press, 1977.

Malbin, Michael J. *Unelected Representatives: Congressional Staff and the Future of Representative Government.* New York: Basic Books, 1980.

Mosher, Frederick D. *The GAO: The Quest for Accountability in American Government.* Boulder, CO: Westview Press, 1979.

Pois, Joseph. *Watchdog on the Potomac: A Study of the Comptroller General of the United States.* Washington, DC: Washington University Press of America, 1979.

Smith, Darrell H. *The General Accounting Office: Its History, Activities, and Organization.* Baltimore: Johns Hopkins University Press, 1927.

Williams, Walter. *The Congressional Budget Office: A Critical Link in Budget Reform.* Seattle: University of Washington, 1974.

Glossary

Act. Legislation that has cleared both houses of Congress and has been signed by the president, or passed over presidential veto, into law.

Amendment. A proposal made by a member of Congress to alter the language, provisions, or stipulations in a bill or in another amendment. An amendment is usually printed, debated, and voted in the same manner as a bill.

Bill. A legislative proposal before Congress. Bills are designated either by "HR" or "S," depending on whether they originated in the House or the Senate and by a number assigned in the order in which they are introduced during the two-year period of a congressional term. *Public bills* deal with general questions and become public laws if approved by Congress and signed by the president. *Private bills* concern individual matters such as claims against the government, immigration and naturalization cases, or land titles, and become private laws if approved and signed.

Bills introduced. A bill that is officially presented for consideration. In both the House and Senate, any number of members may join in introducing a single bill or resolution. The first member listed is the sponsor of the bill, and all subsequent members are the bill's cosponsors. Many bills are committee bills and are introduced under the name of the committee or subcommittee chair. All appropriations bills fall into this category. A committee frequently holds hearings on a number of related bills and may agree to one of them, or to an entirely new bill.

Bills referred. A bill that is referred to the committee or committees that have jurisdiction over the subject under consideration. Both House and Senate rules require that bills be referred by the Speaker (in the House) and the presiding officer (in the Senate). In practice, however, House and Senate parliamentarians refer the vast majority of bills.

Budget. The document sent to Congress by the president early in the year that offers estimates of government revenue and expenditures for the ensuing fiscal year.

Calendar. An agenda or list of business awaiting possible action by each chamber. The House uses five legislative calendars. In the Senate, all legislative matters reported from committee go on a single calendar, listed in the order in which committees report them or they are placed on the calendar by the Senate. Legislative business may be called up out of order by the majority leader, either by obtaining unanimous consent of the Senate or by a motion to call up a bill. The Senate also uses one nonlegislative calendar to handle treaty matters and nominations.

Chamber. The meeting place for the membership of either the House or the Senate; also, the membership of the House or Senate meeting as such.

Committee. A division of the House or Senate that prepares legislation for action by the parent chamber or undertakes investigations as directed by the parent chamber. There are several types of committees. Most standing committees are divided into subcommittees, which study legislation, hold hearings, and report bills, with or without amendments, to the full committee. Only the full committee can report legislation for action by the House or Senate.

Concurrent resolution. Designated "H Con Res" or S Con Res," a concurrent resolution is adopted by both houses but is *not* sent to the president for approval and therefore does not have the force of law. Concurrent resolutions are used, for example, to fix the time for adjournment of a Congress, as a means by which to express Congress's view on a foreign policy or domestic issue, and as a vehicle for coordinated decisions on the federal budget under the 1974 Congressional Budget Act.

Congressional Record. The daily, printed account of proceedings in both the House and Senate chambers, containing substantially verbatim debate and statements and a record of floor action. Highlights of legislative and committee action are embodied in the "Daily Digest" section, while members' extraneous remarks are printed in an appendix entitled "Extension of Remarks." Members may edit and revise remarks made on the floor during debate; hence, quotations from debate reported by the press are not always included. The *Record* allows the reader to distinguish remarks made on the floor from material contained in undelivered speeches. In the Senate, all speeches, articles, and other matter inserted into the *Record* by members who have not actually read that material on the floor are set off by large black dots, or bullets, though a loophole allows members to avoid bulleting if *any portion* of the speech is delivered on the floor. In the

House, undelivered speeches and other material are printed in a distinctive typeface.

Executive calendar. This is a nonlegislative calendar in the Senate on which presidential documents such as treaties and nominations are listed.

Executive Document. A document, usually a treaty, sent to the Senate by the president for consideration. Such documents are referred to committee in the same manner as other measures. Unlike legislative documents, however, treaties do not die at the end of a congress but remain alive until they are either acted on by the Senate or withdrawn by the president.

Hearings. Committee sessions used for taking testimony from witnesses. At hearings on legislation witnesses usually include specialists, government officials, and spokespersons for individuals or entities affected by the bill or bills under study. Hearings related to special investigations bring forth a variety of witnesses. Committees sometimes use their subpoena power to summon reluctant witnesses. The public and press may attend open hearings but are barred from closed, or "executive," hearings. The vast majority of hearings are open to the public.

House calendar. A listing for action by the House of public bills that do not directly or indirectly appropriate money or raise revenue.

Joint resolution. Joint resolutions, designed "H J Res" or "S J Res," require the approval of both houses of Congress and the signature of the president to acquire the force of law. There is no practical difference between a bill and a joint resolution. A joint resolution generally is used to deal with a limited matter, such a single appropriation. Joint resolutions are also used to propose amendments to the Constitution. In these cases, no presidential signature is required. An amendment becomes a part of the Constitution only when three-fourths of the states have ratified it.

Journal. The official record of the proceedings of the House and Senate. The *Journal* offers a record of the actions taken in each chamber. Unlike the *Congressional Record*, however, it does not include a substantially verbatim report of speeches, debates, and statements.

Law. An act of Congress that has been signed by the president or been passed over a presidential veto by Congress. Public bills, when signed, become public laws, and are cited by the letters "PL" and a hyphenated number. The number preceding the hyphen corresponds to the Congress, while the one or more digits after the hyphen refer to the numerical sequence in which the president signed the bill during that Congress. Private bills, when signed, become private laws.

Legislative veto. A procedure that permitted the House and the Senate to review proposed executive branch regulations or actions and to block or modify those with which they disagreed. Congress generally provided for a legislative veto by including in a bill a provision that administrative rules or action taken to implement the law were to go into effect at the end of a designated period of time, unless blocked by either or both houses of Congress. Another version of the veto provided for congressional reconsideration and rejection of regulations already in effect. The Supreme Court in 1983 struck down the legislative veto as an unconstitutional violation of the lawmaking procedure provided in the Constitution.

Override a veto. If the president disapproves a bill and sends it back to Congress with objections, Congress may try to override the veto and enact the bill into law. The override of a veto requires a recorded vote with a two-thirds majority of those present and voting in each chamber. Neither house is required to attempt an override.

Report. The process of reporting to the parent chamber the findings and recommendations of a committee that has been examining a bill. Also, the document setting forth the committee's explanation of its action. Senate and House reports are numbered separately and are designated "S Rept" or "H Rept." When a committee report is not unanimous, the dissenting committee members may file a statement of their views, called minority or dissenting views and referred to as a minority report. Members in disagreement with some provisions of a bill may file additional or supplementary views. Sometimes a bill is reported without a committee recommendation. Adverse reports occasionally are submitted by legislative committees. However, when a committee is opposed to a bill, it usually fails to report the bill at all. Some laws require that a committee report, favorably or otherwise.

Resolution. Designated "H Res" or "S Res," simple resolutions deal with matters entirely within the prerogative of one house or the other. They do no require passage by the other chamber or approval by the president, and do not have the force of law. Most resolutions deal with the rules or procedures of the chamber in which they originate. In the House, a simple resolution is the vehicle for a rule from the Rules Committee. They are also used to express the sentiments of the chamber for such diverse purposes as extending condolences to the family of a deceased member or to comment on foreign policy or executive business.

Slip laws. The first official publication of a bill that has been enacted and signed into law. Each is published separately in unbound, single sheet or pamphlet form.

Statutes at large. A chronological arrangement of the laws enacted in each session of Congress. Though indexed, the statutes are not arranged by subject matter, and there is no indication of how they may have changed previously enacted laws.

Treaties. Executive proposals in the form of resolutions of ratification that must be submitted to the Senate for approval by two-thirds of the members present. Treaties are normally sent to the Foreign Relations Committee for scrutiny before the Senate takes action. Foreign Relations has jurisdiction over all treaties, regardless of subject matter. Treaties are read three times and debated on the floor in much the same manner as legislative proposals. After Senate approval, treaties are formally ratified by the president.

U.S. Code. A consolidation and codification of the general and permanent laws of the United States arranged by subject under fifty titles. The first six deal with general or political subjects; the remainder are alphabetically arranged from agriculture to war. The U.S. Code is updated annually, and a new set of bound volumes is published every six years.

Veto. Executive disapproval of a bill or joint resolution, other than one that proposes an amendment to the Constitution. When Congress is in session, the president must veto a bill within ten days (excluding Sundays) of its receipt; otherwise, the bill becomes law without his signature. When the president vetoes a bill, he returns it to the house of origin along with a message stating his objections.

Author Index

Title Index